SUNDAY ADELAJA

WHY YOU NEED TO URGENTLY BECOME A WORKAHOLIC

Sunday Adelaja

WHY YOU NEED TO URGENTLY BECOME A WORKAHOLIC

©2017 Sunday Adelaja

ISBN 978-1-908040-63-3

Cover design by Oleksandr Bondaruk

Interior design by Adeola Disu

© Sunday Adelaja, 2017,

WHY YOU NEED TO URGENTLY BECOME A WORKAHOLIC

— Milton Keynes, UK:
Golden Pen Limited, 2017

CONTENTS

CHAPTER 5   97

TALENT IS NOT ENOUGH, HARD WORK MAKES THE DIFFERENCE... 97

CHAPTER 6   119

IN SEARCH OFWORKAHOLICS. DO YOU KNOW ANY?...........119

CHAPTER 7   135

FOR THE WORKAHOLIC, LIFE IS PREDICTABLE.....................135

INTRODUCTION

Dear friends, our world is made up of two contrasting groups of people, the rich and the poor, the small and the great, the successful and the failures, the celebrities and the mediocre. You and I fall into either of these groups. Every one of us belong to either the first group or the second in the list. Today there are countries that are known to be the advanced countries of the world while others are known as developing nations. This divide has led to no small amount of devastation, havoc, ruin and wreckages, both in developing countries and in the first world countries. The reason for such a divide is not because it was meant to naturally happen that way. The reason for the contrasting groups is simply because those in the first group know a secret that the other group either does not know or has failed to acknowledge. Have you ever imagined why Michael Jordan was the best basketball player in the world or why Usain Bolt is the fastest man on earth? Have you ever asked yourself why Aliko Dangote is the richest man in Africa but not you or your father?

The reason for all of the contrast is just the knowledge or ignorance of a secret. And that secret is simply a word called WORK. Those who have become great and successful have only become great and successful because they decided to be friends with Work and became known as Workaholics. Those who have become failures and mediocre have only become that because they chose to run away from work. Unfortunately, that same work they ran away from is the number one thing they need to succeed in life. Work is a gift that has been given to man to elevate him to the top. Work is the gift of God to man to make him great. Every man was born great. No man was born greater than another. No man was born more successful than another. Everyone who has become greater than you today is greater than you because he worked harder than you. If there is anyone in life you think is better or more successful than you, it is because such a one became a workaholic. I believe you have what it takes to become successful in life. I believe you have what it takes to become great and be celebrated in the world. You even have the ability to become as financially wealthy as you want. It is possible and it is achievable. That is why I have written this book to challenge you to urgently become a workaholic. I invite you to read this book as it will show you the secrets of success and greatness in life. What I seek to achieve through this book is to teach you how you could become great by applying a simple principle: the principle of hard work. This principle works for both individuals and for nations. Through hard work individuals become great and so do nations.

Never before has anyone imagined that the solutions to a nation's economic crisis and the poverty of its citizens could be hidden in a book. Yet hidden within the pages of this book is the solution to Nigeria's economic crisis. Yet within the pages of this book is the solution to the problem of underdevelopment in the third world countries. I do not know if there is anyone who desires to get to the top of his career and become the best in whatever he does, but within this book are the practical steps to achieving that. I dare you to read this book till the end if you desire to move from the state of small to great, from poor to rich, from mediocre to celebrity and from failure to success, because within its pages are principles that could turn your situation around for good. Read on dear friends and you will soon realize that there is a champion within you.

CHAPTER 1

....

BECOME A LOVER
OF WORK

WHO IS A WORKAHOLIC?

Dear friends, the title of this book is "Why you need to urgently become a Workaholic" But not too many persons know who a workaholic is. When people hear the word workaholic, they don't fully understand what it means. You may not know the meaning of the word "Workaholic" but you might know the meaning of the word alcoholic. An alcoholic is someone who can't function without alcohol. That is to say, he has become so dependent on drinking alcohol that he basically cannot function without it. So if an alcoholic doesn't drink a day, he feels so bad that he begins to have headaches, finds himself out of place in life, feels pains, and develops withdrawal symptoms. An alcoholic is just somebody who has to drink to feel normal and who without drinking has everything just begins to go horrible for him.

Just in the same manner an alcoholic drinks to get the energy for life, so it is with the same terminology that was coined into Workaholic. A Workaholic is not coming from an alcoholic but work + -aholic. It is simply saying that, you also will be a dependant on work as much as a drinker depends on alcohol.

According to Cambridge dictionary, a workaholic is a person who works a lot of the time and finds it difficult not to work.

We could infer from the definitions above, that a workaholic is anyone who cannot function without work. If you must become a workaholic, you will have to so love work that you become addicted to it. If you become addicted to work, you cannot live a day without working. Any day you are not able to work, you will feel so bad and depressed like something bad happened to you. If you can feel comfortable a day without work, then you are not yet a workaholic. I know we live in a nation where everybody is waiting for the weekend or any public holiday so as to not go to work. That attitude is a sign that my country, Nigeria is void of workaholics or maybe has only a few of them. It is in such a country as Nigeria that you will find people praying almost every day of the week asking God for a miracle that will make them successful and great in life. We hate hard work, yet are asking God to give us that which only hard work can give. Only men who love hard work are entitled to success in life. Success and greatness in life are gotten, only thanks to hard work. If a nation must become prosperous, its citizens must of necessity become workaholics. If you as an individual must excel in life and achieve greatness, you cannot but become a workaholic.

PASSION FOR HARD WORK

Almost all the great and successful people in history became great because they developed a passion for hard work. One example of such men who became successful in life because of their passion for hard work is a man by the name Li Ka-shing. Perhaps one of the most important factors that have contributed to Li's success is the passion he feels for his work. In 2010, he told Forbes, "The most important enjoyment for me is to work hard and make more profit."

One of the richest men in Asia and a dominant figure in Hong Kong's economy, Li Ka-Shing started outworking everybody as a teenager en route to building an empire worth billions of US dollars. His net worth as at April 2016 was $27.1 billion

By age 15 Ka-Shing had left school and was working in a plastics factory. He told Forbes how he quickly became a salesman, outsold everybody else, and became the factory's general manager by 19. In 1950, he started his own business and did almost everything, including the accounting, all by himself.

Li Ka-shing was saddled with financial responsibility from a young age. After his family fled to Hong Kong from southern China during WWII, his father died of tuberculosis. He had to leave school before the age of 16 to work in a factory.

For almost four years during the Japanese occupation of Hong Kong, he sent 90% of his pay to his mother. Perhaps his early success as a breadwinner taught him the generous values that have made him famous for his philanthropy today.

Li was clearly influenced by his experience of working as a child. "It doesn't matter how strong or capable you are; if you don't have a big heart, you will not succeed," he said.

Li showed promise as a leader and visionary when he opened his first factory in 1950, at the age of 22. The factory, Cheung Kong Industries, manufactured plastic flowers. He anticipated that plastics would become a booming industry, and he was right.

Though Li dropped out of school at a young age and never received a university degree, he has always been a voracious reader and attributes much of his success to his ability to learn independently. For instance, he completed Cheung Kong's accounting books in the company's first year himself with no accounting experience — he simply taught himself from textbooks.

Wow! How do you explain such success at an early age if not love for hard work? No miracle would have made Li Ka-Shing great and successful if he didn't start working hard at the age of 15 after he dropped out from school. No miracle can make you successful in life if you refuse to work hard. If his love for hard work did not propel him to outwork and outsell everyone else, he could not have become a manager at age 19. How many teenagers do you know in Nigeria or Africa who are managers of factories? What were you doing with your life at the age of 15? I am pretty sure you were still depending on your parents and feeding from mama's kitchen. I am sure you were still watching African magic movies and Premiere league with your life at that age. Your current status in life could tell everyone else what you did with your past years as a teenager or young adult. Your current status in life is always an indicator of how hard working or slothful you were in the past. Hard work always speaks and reveals whether or not you wasted your life in slothfulness in the past. There was practically no way a boy who dropped out from school could rise to such height of success in life if he was not a workaholic. There was no way he could learn accounting by himself without love for hard work. Those who are even privileged to go to school and be taught by teachers still find it difficult to study and understand, yet a boy with no school nor teacher could finish a company's accounting book just by teaching himself from the textbooks. That shows a very high level of love and passion for hard work. Li Ka-shing is no doubt a workaholic and thanks to that he became a successful business man.

The fact that he lost his father to tuberculosis at an early age did not deter him from working hard to succeed. He didn't allow depression to take over his life. He, instead of using his father's death as an excuse for laziness like many other people would do, was rather propelled by it to become a workaholic. He didn't lament and blame everyone else neither did he use his father's death as an excuse to live the life of a mediocre. His love for hard work propelled him forward and made him independent at such an early age. Hard work made him a responsible bread winner after his father's death. He was reported to have sent his salary back home to his mother during those early years of hard work.

I will not fail to draw your attention to the fact that Li Ka-Shing was a voracious reader and self- taught learner. His hard working nature made him read all the books there was to read all by himself. In fact he attributed his success in life to his ability to learn independently. One of the characteristics of workaholics is that they do everything possible to keep learning whether there is a teacher or not. Hard working people become their own teachers. They strive to teach themselves and usually love studying. Show me a man who is a voracious reader and I will show you a man who will become successful in whatever he does. Workaholics will succeed no matter the huddles they face in life.

Along with knowledge and industry insight, Li considers loyalty and reputation to be keys to success. In a 2006 interview with Forbes, he said, "Anytime I say 'yes' to someone, it is a contract." In 1956, he once turned down an offer that would have given him an extra 30% profit on a sale (and allowed him to expand his factory) because he had already made a verbal agreement with another buyer. He still carries this principle of loyalty today, even when it means losing money.

Li's first visionary move was with plastics, though he was ahead of the curve again when he moved into property development in 1979 with the acquisition of Hutchison Whampoa. This set the stage for him to become a major real-estate tycoon before Hong Kong's global boom.

Though he is known mainly as a property developer, Li's company controls 70% of port traffic and most electric utilities and telecommunications in Hong Kong. He also owns a majority stake in Husky Energy, a Canadian company. Li distributes his wealth and power across different industries and geographic areas, showing that he is unafraid to learn and experiment in new arenas.

Though he has many holdings, the thriftiness that was necessary during Li's childhood has carried over into his current career.

Li was one of the first big investors in Facebook and more recently invested in a startup that aims to replace eggs with a plant substitute. Li enjoys spending his "mad money" on these investments rather than on material things. He consciously makes an effort to be perceived as materially modest. He wore a £30 electric wristwatch throughout the 1990s.

Li has no timetable in place for his retirement. The recent consolidation of his holdings into two companies appears to be a move in preparation for when he hands his empire over to his oldest son, Victor. However, at 87-years-old, Li shows no signs of slowing his success anytime soon.

Dear friends, the story speaks for itself. I am sure you need no further proof to believe that being a workaholic is the best thing you could do for yourself if you really desire success and greatness in life. All of Li Ka-Shing's success is thanks to hard work. He became the richest man in Hong Kong and the second richest person in Asia because he became a workaholic. His greatness is thanks to his hard-working lifestyle. Even at the age of 87, he still expresses the attitude of hard work. With the number of companies and investments he has, one will have no reason to doubt that he is a workaholic.

Why did I share this story with you? It is so that you will learn to become great through hard work. My desire is to bring to your consciousness that you can become whatever you want to become if only you will become a workaholic. I wrote this story here for you so that you will know that those who have become great and successful in life only got to that height through hard work. There was never a man in history who became a workaholic who did not succeed in life. Through hard work, all your dreams and aspirations in life can become reality.

"A dream doesn't become reality through magic; it takes sweat, determination and hard work."

COLIN POWELL

No matter how many dreams and ambitions you have, until you become a workaholic, you can never achieve them. It takes hard work, sweat and determination to rise to greatness in life. Everybody can dream dreams but only those who are workaholics will achieve their dreams and faster than everyone else. Therefore I urge you to urgently become a workaholic if you desire to be the best among equals. Become a lover of hard work if you want to become exceptionally successful in life. Hard work worked for Li Ka-Shing and it can work for you too if you become a friend to hard work. Hard work always pays off in the end.

I would like us to draw out a few conclusions from the life of Li Ka-Shing that made him successful.

- He was a hard worker
- He was a voracious reader
- He was a self –taught leaner
- He was a self-motivated individual
- He was a lover of work
- He was a visionary
- He was independent
- He was responsible
- He was a philanthropist
- He was an investor
- He was a man of integrity

- He was materially modest.

- He was thrift and not wasteful

Dear friends, if you desire to be as successful and wealthy as Li- Ka Shing, begin to think hard work. Look at the list of virtues I listed above and begin to cultivate each one of them into your life. Work hard to become all that I listed about the life of Li Ka-Shing if you really desire to be great and successful. Become a hard worker and make sure you strive to learn, read and study every day. That is the first step to greatness. Do not wait for a teacher, become your own teacher. Become your own school. Become a friend to books and libraries. Do not wait for someone else to motivate you to work hard, motivate yourself and keep pushing yourself forward in life no matter the circumstances that come your way. Li lost his father but that didn't stop him from working hard. He didn't allow his father's death to become a setback for him to fail in life but overcame that obstacle through hard work and through it rose to greatness.

> *"Live the Life of Your Dreams. When you start living the life of your dreams, there will always be obstacles, doubters, mistakes and setbacks along the way. But with hard work, perseverance and self-belief there is no limit to what you can achieve."*
>
> ROY T. BENNETT

Love hard work and never detest it. It is the secret of all successes. Be passionate about work such that you cannot live a day without it. One of the things you notice about workaholics is that they are responsible people. They are quick at taking responsibilities. They do not live in irresponsibility and become liabilities. No! Successful people take responsibility for their lives. They do not allow their greatness to be dependent on someone else. They do not blame other people or circumstances for whatever happens in their lives. They take charge of their destiny and become responsible for their failures or successes. We could also notice from the story that Li Ka-Shing was a philanthropist. He didn't accrue material wealth for himself but chose to help others who are in need. He gave out liberally to the poor and needy. He understood that one of the primary reasons for working hard to become wealthy is to have enough to give to those in need. One other thing you could notice from Li's life was that he was an investor. Nobody has truly become successful in business without investments. If you want to be a financial success, you too must learn to invest. Truly great and successful people like Li Ka- Shing are people of integrity. When they say yes, it is yes. If you are a trustworthy person, everyone will want to do business with you. The last thing about Li's life was that he was materially modest. He was not materialistic. He was not extravagant and wasteful in spending. He learnt to save and invest than to waste money on frivolities like most lazy people do. People who understand how to work hard to get money do not spend money anyhow. Only Lazy people who do not understand how much work is done to get money, squander it if it gets to them by chance.

The life of Li Ka-Shing is an example for you and anyone else who desires greatness to emulate.

A Harvard Business School article summarises Li's career in the following way:

From his humble beginnings in China as a teacher's son, a refugee, and later as a salesman, Li provides a lesson in integrity and adaptability. Through hard work, and a reputation for remaining true to his internal moral compass, he was able to build a business empire that includes: banking, construction, real estate, plastics, cellular phones, satellite television, cement production, retail outlets (pharmacies and supermarkets), hotels, domestic transportation (sky train), airports, electric power, steel production, ports, and shipping

Li's businesses cover almost every facet of life in Hong Kong, from electricity to telecommunications, from real estate to retail, from shipping to the Internet. The Cheung Kong Group's market capitalisation is HK$1,193 billion (US$154 billion) as of April 2016. (This includes the Group's controlling stake in 15 listed companies around the world.) The Group operates in over 50 countries and employs around 300,000 staff worldwide.

Having seen the success story and characteristics that made Li Ka- Shing successful, I now encourage you to imbibe and practise these virtues if you really want to become successful in life. Urgently become a workaholic and your story will be read as "a man who through hard work rose from rags to riches, from poverty to affluence" Love hard work and it will propel you to greatness.

HARD WORK: THE FIRST PREREQUISITE FOR SUCCESS

"The three great essentials to achieve anything worthwhile are, first, hard work; second, stick-to-itiveness; third, common sense."

THOMAS EDISON

Thomas Alva Edison was born on February 11, 1847, in Milan, Ohio. He was the last of the seven children of Samuel and Nancy Edison. Thomas's father was a political activist while his mother was an accomplished school teacher. He suffered an early bout of scarlet fever and ear infections which resulted in hearing difficulties in both ears, and eventually left him nearly deaf as an adult.

In 1854, the family moved to Michigan, where Edison spent the rest of his childhood. He went to school only a short time. He did so poorly and was regarded as a difficult child by his teacher. He couldn't cope with school and he was withdrawn to be taught at home by his mother, a former teacher. He learned to love reading, a habit he kept for the rest of his life. He also liked to make experiments in the basement. All through his life, he was a hard worker who devoted most of his time into experimenting and giving birth to inventions. He invested his time working all night most times such that he was able to invent and develop products like the telegraph, phonograph, the electric light bulb, alkaline storage batteries and Kinetograph (a camera for motion pictures).

All through his life he built several laboratories and workshops and employed several workers. But the question is "How was he able to invent and develop all these products?" The answer was simply his love for work. He knew that without work nothing could be invented or produced.

Thomas Edison goes into his workshop and works relentlessly until he forgets time. He could go into his workshop on Monday and work till Friday without knowing that five days have passed. When they come to remind him that it's Friday already, he will argue that it's just the next day thinking that he's just been there for two days. Only a man who is a lover of work could work so much so that he becomes unaware of time. Hard work was the key to all of his inventions. He became a great name in history, thanks to hard work.

"I never did anything worth doing entirely by accident.... Almost none of my inventions were derived in that manner. They were achieved by having trained myself to be analytical and to endure and tolerate hard work."

THOMAS EDISON

From his words, you could see that all of his inventions were born out of his ability to endure and tolerate hard work. Because of his love for work, he was always in that workshop experimenting and inventing things. He lost touch with the environment outside his laboratory that they would break the door to get him out. That was because he understood that to achieve anything of worth in life, hard work is a prerequisite.

It is true that so many people desire to become great achievers in life, however only a few truly love hard work.

No matter how strong your desire to achieve anything in life is, until you become a lover of work, nothing can be achieved. There is no great or successful person today or in history who was not a lover of hard work. From Thomas Edison to Li Ka-Shing, to Michelangelo, to Beethoven and from Michael Jordan to Mark Cuban, to Serena Williams, to Tiger woods and the likes, one thing is common with every one of them; that is the fact that they all became lovers of work. They all were workaholics.

To become a great achiever, you have no other option than becoming a lover of work like the great and successful names listed above. Until you begin to enjoy work, you can never become a great achiever like Thomas Edison. You could see the proof of his love for work in his words below.

"Personally, I enjoy working about 18 hours a day. Besides the short catnaps I take each day, I average about four to five hours of sleep per night"
THOMAS EDISON

Did you see that! 18 hours of work per day! You cannot desire to be great when you can't even focus on 8 hours of work a day. If you want to be as great as Thomas Edison you should also be ready to love work and invest as much time into working as he did. One of the secrets that made Thomas Edison successful was that he enjoyed working for long hours and that was possible because of his love for work. Hard work is the prerequisite for success and without it no one can become truly successful.

Because of his love for work, he got so consumed with his experiments that he lost count of time. He didn't need to check time because he loved working and could invest his life into that work until he got the results he was looking for.

Dear friends, can you work 18 hours a day? If your answer is No, then you have not become a lover of work yet. You are perhaps among those who cannot even work for 8 hours a day without checking time and wanting to stop. In the nearest future, those who have become lovers of work now will rule over those who hate to work. It won't be long before those who have become workaholics dominate over those who have chosen the path of slothfulness. If you must rule and reign in life there must be some form of work for which you have developed love.

For Edison, "that work" was his invention. He was legendary for working almost round the clock, sometimes working over 18 hours every day just to give birth to his inventions. Let me ask you a few questions: do you really want to become great and successful? Are you ready to pay the price for that success? If your answer is yes, then I charge you to become a workaholic. I implore you to work harder than anyone else in what you do. While the whole world is asleep, be awake and work. Before the world will awake from sleep, you would have added value to yourself, you would have invented and produced a product for which the sleeping world would be ready to pay. Those who work more hours than others will rule over those who sleep away their greatness and destiny.

Until his death on October 18, 1931{at age 84}, he was known as someone who worked so hard and made sure that he didn't waste his time sleeping like the rest of the world. Thomas Edison, hated sleep and believed it was a waste of time and did as little of it as possible.

Before his death, everyone had heard of the "Wizard" and looked up to him but that was only thanks to his love for hard work. Because he became a lover of work, the whole world called him a genius.

By the time he died he was one of the most well-known and respected Americans in the world. He had been at the forefront of America's first technological revolution and set the stage for the modern electric world.

Dear friends, my question to you is; do you want to be a great achiever that the world would crave to reckon with? If your answer is yes, then you cannot but learn from Thomas Edison. You must learn to love work like he did. You must learn to become a lover of work and through hard work impact the world with your skills, products and inventions. The secret of all successful people is hard work. To become successful, you will have to stop running away from hard work and learn to start embracing it. Get into your laboratory, your library, your office or workshop and begin to practise hard work. It won't be long before the world will hear your name as one of the geniuses that exist in that field of influence. Thomas Edison became great because he was a workaholic. You too can become great by becoming a workaholic.

You could see from the earlier definition of workaholic "a workaholic is a person who works a lot of the time and finds it difficult not to work" that Thomas Edison was a workaholic because he enjoyed working 18 hours every day. Now look at that definition and ask yourself if you are a workaholic or if you work like Thomas Edison did. I can guess your answer will be "No". If however I asked if you want to become great, you would probably say yes. You see, that is where the problem lies, everybody wants to become great but nobody wants to be a workaholic. There is truly no greatness without first becoming a workaholic. There is truly no genuine wealth without first becoming a workaholic. Hard work is the prerequisite for greatness and without it greatness is impossible.

Dear friends, what did you learn from the life of Thomas Edison? You probably would have learnt that:

- He was a workaholic
- He loved hard work
- He worked almost round the clock, 18hrs a day
- He endured and tolerated hard work
- He loved reading and experimenting
- He hated sleep and saw it as a waste of time
- He knew the value of time

As I bring this chapter to a close, I want you to look at the life of Thomas Edison and apply all the principles that made him great and successful and remember that chief among them was his love for hard work. The same is true for Li Ka- Shing. To replicate the success story of Thomas Edison and Li Ka- Shing, you must urgently become a workaholic like they were. Because only through hard work can greatness, success and wealth be gotten.

NUGGETS FROM
CHAPTER ONE

1. A workaholic is anyone who cannot function without work. If you must become a workaholic, you will have to so love work that you become addicted to it.

2. If you become addicted to work, you cannot live a day without working. Any day you are not able to work, you will feel so bad and depressed like something bad happened to you.

3. Only men who love hard work are entitled to success in life. Success and greatness in life are gotten, only thanks to hard work.

4. If a nation must become prosperous, its citizens must of necessity become workaholics.

5. If you as an individual must excel in life and achieve greatness, you cannot but become a workaholic

6. No miracle can make you successful in life if you refuse to work hard.

7. Your current status in life could tell everyone else what you did with your past years as a teenager or young adult.

8. Your current status in life is always an indicator of how hard working or slothful you were in the past.

9. One of the characteristics of workaholics
   is that they do everything possible to keep
   learning whether there is a teacher or
   not. Show me a man who is a voracious
   reader and I will show you a man who will
   become successful in whatever he does.

10. Workaholics will succeed no matter
    the huddles they face in life.

PRINCIPLES FROM
CHAPTER ONE

1. Those who have become great and successful in life only got to that height through hard work.

2. There was never a man in history who became a workaholic who did not succeed in life.

3. Through hard work, all your dreams and aspirations in life can become reality.

4. No matter how many dreams and ambitions you have, until you become a workaholic, you can never achieve them.

5. It takes hard work, sweat and determination to rise to greatness in life.

6. Everybody can dream dreams but only those who are workaholics will achieve their dreams and faster than everyone else.

7. Become a lover of hard work if you want to become exceptionally successful in life.

8. Become a hard worker and make sure you strive to learn, read and study every day. That is the first step to greatness

9. Love hard work and never detest it. It is the secret of all successes.

10. One of the things you notice about workaholics

is that they are responsible people. They are quick at taking responsibilities. They do not live in irresponsibility and become liabilities

CHAPTER 2

....

WITHOUT WORK
THERE IS NO LIFE

D ear friends, I am glad you proceeded to the second chapter of this book. I hope you learnt in the first chapter that to achieve success in life you must develop love for work. You must become a hard worker who detest laziness. You saw from the last chapter that Thomas Edison was a workaholic and so was Li Ka-Shing. In this chapter, I will reveal to you how work relates to life and how going on vacations can hinder your greatness. This chapter will also explain why most church people are lazy and how the church is raising a slothful multitude. Enjoy the read as we proceed on this adventure.

WORK SUSTAINS LIFE

Work is related to life. Without work there will be no life. It was because God worked that you were created. You are a product of work. Everything that exists is a product of work. Without work nothing can be given birth to. Without work you will have no food to eat because someone is working to produce the food you eat. Without work you will die of sickness and diseases because there will be no way medicines and drugs can be produced. If there are no doctors working in the hospitals, children cannot be given birth to in the hospitals, patients cannot be treated by doctors and surgeries will not be performed. Without work, there would be no electricity, no internet, no phones, no laptops, and nothing will ever exist. Even the earth itself is in existence because God took six days of work to create it. Therefore to say you don't want to work could be taken to mean that you don't want to exist. This is because without work, nothing exists. You are as good as dead if you are not working. It is only natural to work and be a Workaholic. Can you imagine what would happen to you if your heart stops working? Let's imagine that your kidney cells decide not to work or the hepatocytes in your liver choose to become lazy. I want you to envisage a scenario in which the brain cells and all other neurons in your body refuse to work and send nerve impulses to all other organs in your body. What would happen to you? Will you still be alive today? Dear friends, you will die immediately your organs decide to get lazy and stop working. The reason is because, without work there is no life. Just the way your organs must work hard to sustain your life, so should you also work hard lest you die. Hard work will protect your life and keep you from the harmful effects of laziness. Work is a saviour and provides sustenance for life. No greater explanation could be given on the saving power of work than that offered by Voltaire when he said: "Work keeps at bay three great evils; boredom, vice and need"

To simplify what Voltaire had said above, I would like to interpret it in its simplest form by saying that work protects or saves us from boredom, vice and need. This means that when you decide to become a workaholic, you are deciding to shut the door against boredom, keep vices at a distance and never be in need or lack again. If however, you decide not to work, you are opening up your life for the evil of boredom, inviting the evil of vices and troubles and signing up a friendly deal with the evil called poverty. You endanger your life when you refuse to work. The reason for the vices in society is boredom which is born out of a refusal to work. If people are busy working, they would have no time to be involved in the evils of armed robbery, theft, drug addiction and all other societal vices. The major reason for the needs that exist in society is the refusal of people to work. Poverty is a menace in society which is born out of a refusal to work. A lot of people have died because of poverty but that could be traced to its root cause which is a refusal to work. Dear friends, I believe you can see now, that without work there is no life. Without work there is no sustenance. This is the reason I urge you to urgently become a workaholic. Urgently become a workaholic so as to protect your life from poverty, sickness and diseases. You can enjoy a life of wealth and financial abundance. You can become successful in life but only thanks to your degree of diligence.

WORKAHOLICS DON'T GO ON HOLIDAY

There are a lot of motivational speakers who go about teaching that hard work is harmful and that you should rest rather than work. All of the theories by those motivational speakers that you should not go to work but rather go on vacation is a lie and a deception. The quickest way to endanger your life is to believe the lies that hard work is bad. If vacation is the way to greatness, then why didn't the great men in history live all their lives in vacation? Show me one great man in history who was rewarded for going on vacation. All the great names in history were rewarded and celebrated for their hard work not for going on vacations. They were all busy working hard to see how they could make the world a better place. They all loved hard work and hated vacations.

"I hate vacations. If you can build buildings, why sit on the beach?"

PHILIP JOHNSON

If doctors stop working and go on vacation, what would happen to the health and lives of people all around the world? Just imagine what would happen if those working in the electricity and gas sector all go on vacation and refuse to work. If the farmers and traders refuse to work because they decide to go on vacation, there would be no food and commodities in the market. If everyone in the aviation sector stop working, no one would be able to travel across countries and continents. I could go on listing the tragedy that will happen if we all decide to go on vacation and stop working. Therefore I believe you will agree with me now that without work, there will be no life. It is not life when you are not working. Even in heaven you are going to work. So don't tell me you have gotten to a place where you will never work. It is self -deception. People who are always asking for vacations are lazy people and can hardly become successful in life. I am about to show you the story of a workaholic who didn't live in slothfulness asking for vacations but through hard work became successful.

A MAN WHO DIDN'T GO ON
VACATION FOR SEVEN YEARS

When starting his first company, he routinely stayed up until two in the morning reading about new software, and went seven years without a vacation. His name is Mark Cuban, the owner of Dallas Mavericks

Mark Cuban (born July 31, 1958) is an American businessman, investor, author, television personality, and philanthropist. He is the owner of the National Basketball Association's Dallas Mavericks. Mark Cuban is one of the exceptionally successful American entrepreneurs who has net worth of $3.3 Billion according to the Forbes. Popularly known as "Shark Tank", he lives a life that most people envy. He founded his first company called Micro Solutions and sold it for $6 million to CompuServe in 1995. While starting his first company, Mark Cuban stayed until 2am everyday working and reading about new software and did this for seven years without vacation.

Can you imagine that! That a man could work for seven years without a vacation? No wonder he became successful and wealthy. It was thanks to hard work that he became successful. He was a workaholic who wouldn't go on vacation because of his love and passion for work. If you really want to have a successful life, you will need to become a workaholic urgently. If you are really serious about becoming successful in life, you will convert all your vacations into a time of hard work. While others go on vacation, convert your vacation into a time of work. Make your vacation productive and keep working hard so as to become successful.

He was born in Pittsburgh, Pennsylvania and has always been enthusiastic and sports fanatic. At the age of 12, he was selling garbage bags with the only purpose to buy a new pair of high-end basketball sneakers. However, this dealing sowed the seeds of business dealing to come. Throughout his high school, he continued to work anything like promoting disco parties and bar-tending.

After completing his graduation from Indiana University, he got his first job in the early 80's in a software company named, Your Business Software. During his time in the company, PC's were growing swiftly and he made a handsome relationships with multiple software clients. He started meeting the clients on the side to seek business opportunity to grow his own business. Seeing this, the Company fired him but his clients came with him.

After getting fired from his job, he launched his own company named, Micro Solutions, without wasting any time. The company was based on software reselling which gained a lot of publicity in a very short time. Few years later, in 1990, Cuban sold Micro Solutions to CompuServe for $6 million. After clearing all the taxes, Cuban ended up with $2 million in his pocket. In the mid 90's he was busy trading in stocks. He became an investor and at that point, Cuban had turned his $2 million into $20 million.

His passion for Sports curved into a huge profitable business. In 1998, along with his college friend, Cuban, started another company named, Audionet.com. Both were huge fan of basketball, their business was online portal merging basketball and webcasting. Later on, he changed the company's name to Broadcast.com. The Broadcast.com expanded to over 300 employees and $100 million in annual revenue by late 90's.

Dear friends, I want you to notice something about Mark Cuban, and that is the fact the he is a workaholic. Right from childhood, at age 12, he was already displaying the trait of a workaholic. The fact that he was selling garbage bags at that age suggests to me that he was not a lazy child. Again, while in high school, he was also working and schooling. He could do any kind of job that came his way including promoting disco parties and bar tending. One of the proofs that he was a workaholic was the fact that his clients followed him from the company where he was fired to his own company. If he were a lazy guy, nobody would follow him. He founded several companies and that could only be possible because he is hard-working. You could see that all his wealth came to him because he worked hard. If he was going on vacation every day or week, he would not have recorded such success in his businesses.

He loved hard work so much so that he worked almost round the clock. This could be seen in one of his sayings:

> *"Work like there is someone working 24 hours a day to take it away from you"*

The quotation above by Mark Cuban is one that should challenge you to work harder than anyone else. Can you imagine that! Cuban is saying that you should work round the clock because if you don't someone else will do and that person automatically will rule over you tomorrow. In a race everyone runs but only one person wins the race. The harder you work, the more your likelihood of winning in the race of life. Work hard like there is someone else who will get to the finish line before you. Even if everyone else is working hard, you can outwork them all by urgently becoming a workaholic. Mark Cuban has become more successful than his contemporaries because he worked harder than them all.

When dot com was booming, he decided to sell Broadcast.com to Yahoo. Finally, in 1999, Yahoo picked it up for $5.9 BILLION in Yahoo stock. When the deal was officially closed, it was the peak time of dot com and Yahoo's stock was trading at $163 per share.

After six months, when he had full access to his stocks share, he gambled all his shares and dumped entire stake on the open market. Within a week, he sold every single share of Yahoo and was left with $2.5 BILLION in cash to his side.

Today he owns, a basketball team-Dallas Mavericks, Landmark Theatres, film distribution company- Magnolia Pictures, 24,000 square foot mansion in Dallas and a private jet worth $40 million.

Dear friends, today Cuban has a net worth of $3.3 billion and that was thanks to hard work. Don't forget how he got to this stage of his life; it was through hard work. Remember that while starting his first company, Mark Cuban stayed until 2am everyday working and reading about new software and did this for seven years without vacation. He became successful because he refused to go on vacation and rather chose to work hard every day for seven years. If you really want to be wealthy and great, you must work hard even while others go on vacation. To increase your net worth like Cuban has done, you must become a workaholic.

As I summarize Mark Cuban's success story, I would like to review his life and see what virtues you could learn and apply to make you as successful as he is.

- He was a workaholic
- He worked almost round the clock
- He loved working and hated idleness
- He hated vacations
- He was an investor

It is my belief that if you cultivate these virtues in your life, you will become as successful as he is.

THE DECEPTION OF THE MODERN CHURCH

I am not diplomatic particularly on issues relating to what I consider the truth. I say it the way I feel it should be said. This explains why I am pained that my colleagues have turned their congregations into money making projects for selfish gains. This is how I feel about the Nigerian church presently: "Everybody says Nigeria's problem is about leadership but I disagree with that assertion because a nation gets a leader it deserves. Our leaders are from this country, they were born and grew up within this same environment.

They were not imported from Guinea-Bissau or Ukraine, they were brought up in Nigeria. I think our problem is really not about leadership but our value system.

Three things determine the value of a nation, the family, the educational system and the Church. I mentioned the church because nobody has the opportunity of speaking to over 40 million Nigerians every week like pastors. "When people go to Church, they are not going there for argument. They are obliged to just accept whatever the pastor says even if he is saying rubbish. Even the president of the country does not have the kind of power we have. So, we have a very huge responsibility upon us. Unfortunately, most of us instead of releasing values and information that will facilitate national progress and development, we are talking of breakthrough today, breakthrough tomorrow. What we are cultivating from the pulpit is the culture of instant gratification. We are telling people, raise up your hands if you want to be a millionaire by the end of the year and of course everybody raises up their hands.

These people however are left without an answer as to how they can become millionaires after they raised their hands in church to indicate that desire. This state of oblivion results in raising a group of people who just fold their arms without working but expecting a financial miracle before or at the end of the year. Furthermore, this ideology creates a culture of laziness in the people instead of that of hard work.

Listen to me if you are a pastor reading this book. You must teach the people the process of production, perseverance, endurance and how to work with their hands.

"Miracles could happen but nations don't get developed that way. There is no nation in the world that got developed by miracles. All developed nations got developed thanks to hard work. If we must bring about development in our nation, then our pastors must start teaching hard work instead of miracles"

Again what about the money that is coming to the man before the end of the year, if he gets it without working for it, is it not robbery? Because you have transferred the money from someone who worked to another person who didn't work. That is corruption from the pulpit. That kind of preaching generates the mentality of instant gratification.

Prayers don't develop a nation. It is the work of your hand that does. Look at China, Japan, they don't believe in God, but they are more prosperous than Nigeria. Why? The reason is because they strongly believe in hard work. They are workaholic.

The Japanese who don't believe in God will go to hell if they don't repent, but while here on earth, they will be prosperous whereas Nigerians who are religious will make heaven but while here on earth, will continue to experience the challenges and economic crisis that we are going through now. God does not and will not go back on his words. He said, 'I will diligently reward the works of your hands'.

Dear friends, Prayer does not and cannot develop a nation. We must learn the virtue of hard work if we want our nations to be developed. It is because we are void of the value of hard work as a nation that everybody wants to become financially wealthy without working hard for it. It is in Nigeria that I found out that we don't care to know how a man makes his money, whether he is a ritualist or fraudster, we don't want to know provided we can take from him. What a lack of values!

RAISING A SLOTHFUL MULTITUDE

It is so sad that churches are keeping their people there all the time instead of chasing them to go and work hard. They are sensitising them to wait for miracles instead of teaching them to work hard and become workaholics.

The messages in church should be telling people that, unless they work, their miracles will not come and that it is only through hard work that they can build the desired future they wish for. The life of abundance is only possible to the person who works hard. Unfortunately, we are teaching people to depend on miracles. It is in Nigeria that you see programmes like "24-hour breakthrough programme" even on working days. It is in my country that you see programmes like 30 days miracle service which holds from morning till evening for thirty days. When people should be at their work places, they are rather wasting their time in church praying for a financial miracle. What a mentality! This is how our pastors raise a multitude of slothful people. People who are expecting something for nothing. People who want to become financially buoyant without hard work.

The tragedy however with these people is that they have placed their success in life to be dependent upon their pastor's prophecy. If you are waiting for a prophetic word from your pastor to make you prosperous instead of working hard, I am sorry you are signing in for failure and poverty in life. Instead of hoping for a miracle which you are not certain about, why not urgently become a workaholic? If you become a workaholic, you can be sure of your success and financial prosperity at the end of the year instead of hoping endlessly for a miracle. While others are waiting for an uncertain miracle, you can be certain about how much finances you would make when you work hard. You no longer depend on prophecies and miracles to become rich. You soon realize that those who are waiting for miracles will start coming to you to beg for financial assistance. Being a workaholic places you above the lazy multitude who are waiting for miracles. Refuse to join the slothful multitude. Work hard and be different because it is only through hard work you can build the prosperous future you desire.

Dear friends, another reason why you must become a workaholic is so that you can remove yourself from the influence and deception of selfish pastors. You may be wondering what I mean by that; Well, let me explain it to you. Most pastors in Nigeria are as lazy as their members. Have you asked yourself why churches now organize programmes every day of the week and collect different kind of offerings?

"Every message now in Nigerian churches must end with offering. You give offering for breakthrough, healing, first born, thanksgiving, celebration, and so on and so forth. All these offerings are just to enrich the lazy pastors who have no other source of income and depend only on church offerings for survival. This is so that by the time the people are being impoverished, the pastors are going about in Jeeps and jets. They are the oppressors of this world. All the breakthrough and miracle programmes are dubious methods of extracting the little the people have left. It is day light robbery and they are using the name of God to do it. Run away from such churches and go work hard with your hands and you will no longer be deceived by the numerous parasitic pastors asking you to come for miracle services. Stay away from lazy parasites, who perch on you just to satisfy their needs, they do not come to alleviate your burdens, hence, their mission is to distract, detract and extract, and make you live in abject poverty."

MICHAEL BASSEY JOHNSON

TIGER WOODS: RULING VIA HARD WORK

Tiger Woods was born on December 30 1975. He is considered to be one of the most talented sportsmen ever. He has already been regarded as one of the most successful golfers ever. He is also the highest paid athlete in the world.

For all his achievements, he has been working throughout the years to nurture his talents and try to play at his full potential.

Tiger as many would call him started golf when he was 2years old. He didn't start playing but started imitating his father and replicating the way he would play his strokes. Tiger was a child prodigy.

At the age of 6, he won the under-10 competition at the Navy Golf course, Cypress. At the age of 8, he broke the 80 strokes barrier.

From 1988 to 1991, he won the Junior World Golf Championship. He beat his father who was a golf instructor at the age 11. From then on, Tigers father could never beat him. At the age of 12, Tiger had broken the 70 strokes barrier for the first time. The 70 stroke mark was sometimes out of reach for even experienced amateur golfers. Tiger's father had set his son the target of breaking Jack Nicklaus's records.

Before we continue with the Tiger Woods story, I want us to deliberate briefly on how he became so good that he was able to beat his father and even break the 70 stroke at such an early age. The reason is simply hard work. It is only hard work that can make you better than your teachers and instructors. Tiger became a skilful player because of the amount of hard work and rehearsals he was exposed to. There is nothing you cannot learn or become when you make hard work your life style. Ordinary men have become great through hard work. Ordinary men have become professionals in what they do through hard work. When you become a workaholic, there is nothing you cannot achieve. When you add so much value to yourself through hard work, the whole world will celebrate you and look up to you as a genius.

In 1991, at the age of 15, Tiger became the youngest ever U.S junior amateur champion. He again won the title in 1992 and 1993. In 1994, he won the US amateur championship. He graduated from Western High school in 1994 at the age of 18.

In 1995, he joined Stanford University on a golf scholarship. He participated in 1995 Masters tournament and was tied for the 41st spot. He again won the US amateur championship in 1995 and 1996. Now he had won both the amateur and junior amateur championship three times in a row. In august 1996, he left college and became a professional golfer.

He was named Sports' illustrated 1996 sportsman of the year. He made history in 1997 when he won his first major, the Masters Tournament. Two months later, he became the number 1 player in the world. This was the fastest time in which any golfer had reached that position.

Dear friends did you notice how fast Tiger became the number one player in the world? He got to that position so quickly because he was a workaholic. He became the king of golf because he urgently became a workaholic.

While everyone may want the kind of success that Tiger Woods had, most people, perhaps up to 98%, are not willing to do whatever he did to achieve that. Listen friends, the surest way to success is to apply a simple principle. That is the principle of diligence, the principle of hard work. Yes, your greatest and surest way to success is your ability to work hard and do so consistently. Your greatest source of success in life is hidden in the word "hard work" That was what propelled Tiger woods to the top of his career and can do the same for you and anyone else who decides to apply the principle of diligence.

THE GREATEST PERFORMANCE IN GOLF HISTORY.

In 2000, he was the peak of his powers. He achieved six consecutive wins, the longest winning streak since 1984. At the 2000 U.S open, he broke or tied nine tournament records. Sports illustrated called this the greatest performance in golf history. In the year 2000, he was able to win the last three majors of the year. Tiger at the age of 24 had become the youngest player to achieve the Career Grand Slam. He had won nine of the twenty PGA tournaments he entered in and had reordered the lowest scoring average in PGA tour history.

ACHIEVEMENTS

Woods won the masters tournament and that made him the first player to hold all four majors at the same time. After his superb performances in 2003 and 2004, he was not able to win a major in the next two years. Tiger lost the number 1 position and his dominance over the golf world. Again woods came back into his elements in 2005, winning back his No.1 position and two majors. Again 2006 and 2007 were great years for Tiger. He won three majors and finished second twice.

He continued his form into 2008, where again he finished second in the first major of the year. In the U.S open that year, in spite of having a knee injury, Tiger went on to claim the title. He was applauded by his opponents and the spectators for his determination and willpower.

The 2013 season was a triumphant one for Woods. He won five tournaments, including the Arnold Palmer Invitational, the Farmers Insurance Open and the Players Championship, and was named the PGA Tour Player of the Year for the 11th time.

The secret to success is hard work and that cannot be overemphasized. If you are not successful in what you do, it means you are not working hard. But if you think that you are working as hard as you can but are not successful, then become a workaholic. You will definitely succeed if you do. However, the fact of the matter is that only very few people are ready to work harder than they already are. Not too many persons are willing to go the extra mile, to run a little harder, sweat a little more, train just a little longer, and work a little harder to become successful. Unfortunately, it is that extra commitment that makes the difference. What do you think separates the best from the rest anyway? Do they have more talent than the rest? Not necessarily! Are they more physically gifted than the rest? No sir. They are only more workaholic than you and everyone else. That is the reason for Tiger Woods' success. He worked harder than everyone else in the game of golf and thanks to that he became the star. Anybody who is better than you in whatever you do has only become better because he worked harder than you. If you truly desire to rule your world, I dare you to urgently become a workaholic like Tiger Woods was.

As I bring this chapter to a close, I would like to remind you of the facts and principles that we've learnt in this session. The first thing you must not forget is that without work there would be no life. If you refuse to work, you are sign-ing your death warrant. It is work that sustains life. Fur-thermore we saw how vacation is a thief of time and how it could hinder you from attaining greatness. Mark Cuban became great because he refused to go on vacation and rather worked hard while others went on vacation. Do not forget that it is better to work hard than to depend on mir-acles. Workaholics are always ahead of and more successful than miracle seekers. Finally, I would like to remind you that Tiger woods became successful in his career thanks to hard work. You too can become great and successful by becoming a workaholic and by applying the principles that are in this chapter.

In the next chapter, I am going to be showing you the reasons why nations go into recession and how that can be prevented. You will be amazed at how much of a role you are to play in making your nation prosperous. Join me as we proceed to the next chapter to discover life changing truths and principles.

NUGGETS FROM
CHAPTER TWO

1. Work is related to life. Without work there will be no life.

2. It was because God worked that you were created. You are a product of work. Everything that exists is a product of work. Without work nothing can be given birth to.

3. Therefore to say you don't want to work could be taken to mean that you don't want to exist. This is because without work, nothing exists.

4. You are as good as dead if you are not working. It is only natural to work and be a Workaholic.

5. Just the way your organs must work hard to sustain your life, so should you also work hard lest you die.

6. Hard work will protect your life and keep you from the harmful effects of laziness. Work is a saviour and provides sustenance for life.

7. When you decide to become a workaholic, you are deciding to shut the door against boredom, keep vices at a distance and never be in need or lack again.

8. If however, you decide not to work, you are opening up your life for the evil of boredom,

inviting the evil of vices and troubles and signing up a friendly deal with the evil called poverty. You endanger your life when you refuse to work.

9. If people are busy working, they would have no time to be involved in the evils of armed robbery, theft, drug addiction and all other societal vices.

10. The major reason for the needs that exist in society is the refusal of people to work. Poverty is a menace in society which is born out of a refusal to work. The reason for the vices in society is boredom which is born out of a refusal to work.

PRINCIPLES FROM
CHAPTER TWO

1. If you are waiting for a prophetic word from your pastor to make you prosperous instead of working hard, I am sorry you are signing in for failure and poverty in life.

2. Prayer does not and cannot develop a nation. We must learn the virtue of hard work if we want our nations to be developed.

3. You can become successful in life but only thanks to your degree of hard work.

4. The quickest way to endanger your life is to believe the lies that hard work is bad.

5. All the great names in history were rewarded and celebrated for their hard work not for going on vacations. They were all busy working hard to see how they could make the world a better place. They all loved hard work and hated vacations.

6. People who are always asking for vacations are lazy people and can hardly become successful in life.

7. While others go on vacation, convert your vacation into a time of work. Make your vacation productive and keep working hard so as to become successful.

8. Work round the clock because if you don't someone else will do and that person automatically will rule over you tomorrow.

9. Being a workaholic places you above the slothful multitude who are waiting for miracles.

10. Work hard and be different because it is only through hard work can you build the prosperous future you desire.

CHAPTER 3

WHY NATION GO INTO RECESSION

Have you ever wondered why nations go into recession? Has it crossed your mind why some nations are prospering while others are struggling with recession? I will try to explain that to you in this session. I am also going to be showing you why some nations are prosperous and others are not and the role you have to play in the development of your nation. Read on dear friends!

The number one reason for recession in any nation is laziness. By that I mean the refusal of the citizens of that nation to become workaholics.

Ecclesiastes 10:18a says that, because of laziness, the building decays. Here the building is your life and laziness will bring decay to your life. The roof of your life will collapse and fall in and that is the same thing that will happen to any society. Any society full of lazy people will come to decay sooner or later. In one way or the other, decay will come to the economy, systems, lifestyle, ministries, agencies, institutions and everything else. This particular verse reminds me of my country Nigeria where everything is falling apart because there is no maintenance culture. Anywhere you don't see the culture of maintenance, then there is the culture of laziness. Laziness brings decay, corruption and bad economy.

The second part of Ecclesiastes 10:18 "And through the idleness of hands, the house leaks." That is, the resources of the nation will leak. There is going to be brain drain, economic drain and all kinds of drainage will be going on in the society or country where there is a culture of laziness. So for any country to develop, it has to first of all overcome the culture of laziness in its citizens by teaching them to become workaholics. No matter what you do, if this culture is not overcome, the building of that house or nation will leak and fall in. This is what happens if laziness is not declared a persona-non grata in any society. So for anybody or country to grow, there must be a campaign against laziness. Every developed country has an addiction to work. The system forces them to work. Developed nations are full of workaholics.

HOW TO BECOME A DEVELOPED NATION THROUGH DIGNITY OF LABOUR

Development and civilization is the quest of every nation under the sun. This quest has apparently created a dichotomy in our world. Today there are countries that are known to be the advanced countries of the world while others are known as developing nations. This divide has led to no small amount of devastation, havoc, ruin and wreckages, both in developing countries and in the first world countries.

As many as 700 immigrants were reported drowned in the Mediterranean, just outside Libyan waters, in what is the worst disaster yet involving migrants being smuggled to Europe.

This is the news report that recently went all over the world as the world stood in shock of what could be the reason driving so many young Africans into an early death under such terrible circumstances. That brings the total number of deaths under similar circumstances to 1500 migrants en-route Europe in the first quarter of 2015.

A week earlier, in a similar incident, another 400 young Africans lost their lives in their quest for a better life. As big as this number might seem to us, the scope of disaster could have been much wider. The Italian rescue operation reportedly rescued 100,000 lives of young Africans that could have perished under similar circumstances.

What is driving these young, vibrant, energetic African men from different countries of Africa to so desperately risk their lives? That might be a question to the Europeans or first world nations, but to us Africans it is an obvious question that demands no answer. Every African hypothetically would understand what is driving these young men to desperately want to move to Europe.

On the other side of the world, the United States of America is facing an on-going battle to secure her borders from another group of young, vibrant, energetic illegal immigrants. Only this time they are not from Africa but from Latin American countries.

What do these two groups of young men in the Libyan Mediterranean and the Gulf of Mexico have in common? The answer is obvious, they all want to escape the life of abject poverty in their underdeveloped nations and move onto a dreamed and superlative lifestyle in the advanced nations of the world.

As a result of this quest for a better lifestyle in advanced nations of the world, Africa keeps losing some of her most promising children. Is there anything that could be done? Yes, no doubt there is!

In my opinion, one of the answers to the question of underdevelopment of nations including my country Nigeria is in the CULTURE of DIGNITY OF LABOR.

DIGNITY OF LABOR indicates that all types of jobs are respected equally, and no occupation is considered superior. Though, one's occupation for his or her livelihood involves physical work or menial labour, it is held that the job carries dignity, compared to the jobs that involve more intellect than bodily strength.

One of the major contributions of the Protestant faith to the world is the culture of dignity of labour. At the time Martin Luther, John Calvin and other leaders of the protestant reformation started their works of reformation in Europe, Europe was as backward and as underdeveloped as most countries in Africa are today.

Some of the countries we have now come to respect in Europe like Germany and England were so backward and underdeveloped that Germans were known as lazy drunks who despised any form of hard work. In England, things were so bad that the streets of London had homeless people everywhere dying of poverty, prostitution, alcoholism without any hope of things ever getting better.

> "Hard work spotlights the character of people: some turn up their sleeves, some turn up their noses, and some don't turn up at all."
>
> JOHN CARMACK

When the protestant preachers began delivering their extremely fiery messages in the churches and in the streets of Europe, one of their main focus in preaching was called the dignity of labour, Which entailed the following facts:

- Everybody must get a job.

- All jobs must be respected, because they are being done unto God.

- By working we become co-workers with God.

- Work is a form of service to God.

- No occupation is considered superior since everyone is doing his best where he is.

- You need to work even if it is a menial or dirty job, because every job is participating in the process of creation.

- Everybody must work even if you are not working for money. You must work to actualize yourself.

> "He who has a slack hand becomes poor, but the hand of the diligent makes rich"
>
> PROVERBS 10:4

What did the concept of dignity of labour do to Europe and what can it do to Africa today? What these very commendable efforts of preachers did to Europe is that:

- It took people off the streets.
- People were taught that they were created by God and they themselves must become creators like God.
- There came a respect and dignity for work.
- People began to understand that wealth and success is not a matter of luck.
- Superstition regarding work and wealth was broken. Everybody now knew that wealth comes only from hard work, not from some superstitious beliefs.
- The society was taught to respect all workers.
- Each worker no matter the level knows he is participating in the process of creation with God hence the dignity.
- Every worker knows that by working, he is releasing the nature of God in him. He is becoming creative just like God is creative.
- In the process, factories, industries began to spring up all over the place.
- It led to industrial revolution with 75% of inventions and discoveries being credited to Protestants who were taught in the culture of dignity of labour.

THE GET RICH QUICK MENTALITY

I believe that for Nigeria and other third world countries to truly become developed, we must change the culture and attitude of our people towards work. In my observations, I see that the culture that is prevalent right now in Nigeria and indeed Africa is the culture of GET RICH QUICK. That is why most young people are dreaming of becoming politicians so as to get rich quick. They say it's their turn to eat the national cake. People no longer want to work hard to become successful. Everyone wants to get to the top by hook or by crook. The average Nigerian youth wants to fight his way to the national assembly, not because he has anything good to offer the nation but because he wants to get rich quick by looting the nation's treasury.

> *"The dictionary is the only place that success comes before work. Work is the key to success, and hard work can help you accomplish anything."*
>
> VINCE LOMBARDI

What the culture of get rich quick does to our people is:

- Young men only wish to do prestigious work.
- Our young people look for quick answers and solutions.
- People want to get something for nothing.
- They look down at people who are engaged in manual labour.
- Fraudulent money schemes are prevalent in the society
- Armed robbery, theft becomes the order of the day.
- People don't believe that hard work is worth it.
- People begin to think that there is no natural process to success, hence the fraudulently rich (swindlers,

drug pushers, 419 scammers etc.) begin to become respected in the society

- People forget that they have to create their wealth in their nation. They rather think they must be given.
- The escapist mentality becomes prevalent, giving birth to the syndrome of economic refugees.

> *"The soul of a lazy man desires, and has nothing;*
> *but the soul of the diligent shall be made rich."*
> PROVERBS 13:4

IS WORK A CURSE?

One destructive mind-set that must be altered in our society is the thought that work is a curse. Some people advocate that if you are truly blessed you don't need to work hard. Because as they say the "race is not to the swift", I even had statements like "a day of favour is better than a thousand years of labour". To make things worse, this type of teachings are actually coming from our pulpits. We call ourselves Protestants, but we have totally departed from the teachings of the early Protestants. Martin Luther, John Wesley and John Calvin would turn in their graves, if they hear the kind of teachings we are now feeding the people of God with. A major contributing factor to the recession in our economy is the misconception that work is a curse and unfortunately, this misconception is arising from the modern day church. The churches are telling people that work is a result of the fall of Adam and that it was the curse in Genesis that brought about work. Nothing could be farther from the truth than that assertion. A careful study of the book of Genesis will reveal that God already told Adam to work before the fall of man. Therefore, to say that work is as a result of the fall will be the most misleading statement in the body of Christ. Those preachers who say that because Jesus has come and paid for our sins, that we no longer need to work and that God's grace and favour will make us rich are only displaying their ignorance of scriptures and are therefore propagating a lie. The prevailing belief that it is a curse for a believer to work has therefore done no good to our nation as it has cultivated a culture of laziness in our citizens.

> *"Work is not a curse; it is the prerogative of intelligence, the only means to manhood, and the measure of civilization. "*
>
> CALVIN COOLIDGE

How can work be a curse, when Jesus himself worked? How could we be so deceived into thinking that work is a curse when God himself is still working? Even the apostle Paul encouraged us to work so as to have to give. He said let he that stole steal no more but he should rather work so that he might have enough to give. Even Paul himself worked. Does that mean he was cursed too? You and I know that he was not. We therefore must raise a campaign against the misconception that work is a curse if we must raise a generation of people who will become Workaholics.

IT IS THE CULTURE THAT MAKES THE DIFFERENCE.

What the new government of Nigeria and other African governments must do, is to start a massive reorientation campaign in support of the culture of the dignity of labour. We must bring back dignity to hard work. Our people must once again realize that it is only hard work and excellence that leads to wealth creation.

> *"Wealth gained by dishonesty will be diminished, but he who gathers by labour will increase."*
> PROVERBS 13:11

It must once again become a common knowledge to our people that it is only the wealth that we create that we can share. From our primary schools to secondary schools, to tertiary institutions, there must be a mass campaign to educate our people about the value of labour. We must so stress the importance of hard work that everybody would want to become workaholic.

Every major outward change must first begin in the mind. So for us to expect development in our nations, we must first bring development to the minds and understandings of our people. The change we quest for outwardly must first be attained inwardly.

While they, the early Protestants focused on forming the nature of God in people, the Protestants of today are focused on gratifying the needs of the people. As a result of their teachings, the early Protestants created a new society that we now refer to as developed and advanced countries. It is the descendants of these early European protestants that later scattered throughout the surface of the earth. Everywhere they went, they took the same message and culture of dignity of labour with them.

As a result, these Protestants that moved to Australia brought about a quick and accelerated growth and development. When they went to America with the same work ethic and culture of dignity of labour, America quickly became a developed and advanced nation.

The descendants of these early Protestants took this same culture to South Africa, New Zealand, and everywhere they went, they were able to replicate the same work ethic that resulted in growth and development.

It must be noted however, that there were other Europeans that travelled to other parts of the earth, but because they did not take with them the same Protestant culture of dignity of labour, they did not record the same level of success, growth and development as the early Protestant Immigrants had done.

Examples of these other Europeans that moved from the continent to other continents are the immigration from Spain to Latin American countries. They took with them the Catholic culture. As a result those countries are still developing countries till today. It is the culture that makes the difference. When there is no internal transformation, there cannot be external progress and development whatsoever.

Other Europeans that moved from the mainland Europe were Portuguese, one of the richest countries along with Spain those days, yet because their descendants did not have the same culture of dignity of labour as in the Protestant countries, the Portuguese could not bring about development to Brazil and other Portuguese speaking nations. It is the culture that makes the difference.

Even today in modern Europe, it is a known fact that the most developed countries are the countries with the Protestant tradition, while the dominantly Catholic nations like Spain, Italy and Portugal are less developed.

What I am trying to say is that we must change the minds of our people towards positively relating to work, labour, etc. Our government, media houses, schools, must focus on creating a new culture in our society; A culture of work. A culture of labour. A culture of diligence. A culture of hard work. A culture of perseverance. A culture of persistence. A culture of dignity of labour. Until we teach our people to become workaholics, we cannot bring an end to the recession and the numerous challenges that have plagued us as a nation.

ALLERGIC TO LAZINESS

Dear friends, if our nation must become a developed nation, we must all become allergic to laziness. Until you and I become allergic to laziness, we cannot become workaholics. People who are workaholics are allergic to laziness. They cannot stand laziness because they hate it with a passion. Workaholics have a strong dislike for indolence. Workaholics could even fall sick if there is no work for them to do. To become successful in life, you must become allergic to laziness and develop love for hard work. You have to put the mark of the love for work in your nature such that you become allergic to laziness. This means that, if you are not working, you can't talk to anybody, smile, eat or sleep. That is, you have to get yourself to a point where it is only when you work that you have energy. If you refuse to become allergic to laziness, you will regret the consequences that will follow.

> "I went by the field of the lazy man, And by the vineyard of the man devoid of understanding; and there it was, all overgrown with thorns; its surface was covered with nettles; its stone wall was broken down."
>
> PROVERBS 24:30-31

From the verse above, the field of the lazy man will become overgrown with thorns. Your life will be overgrown with thorns if you refuse to become a workaholic. Your life will be broken in pieces if you are not allergic to laziness. Laziness will destroy your life and endanger your future. Hard work will rescue you from a life of oblivion. Hard work is a key to subduing your Promised Land. Lazy people cannot subdue their promise lands. Anyone who does not work disgraces himself and steals from the wealth of those who do labour.

If a man does not work, he gives nothing of value to the world. He is a thief and useless to God.

Our laziness as a nation has been fuelled recently by fraudulent money schemes like MMM. MMM means mavrodi mondial movement, it is simply a social community where people come together to help one another financially.

My concern about MMM and all such fraudulent money schemes is that it will destroy the future of our country and the reason I say that is because what these schemes are doing is to invite people to neglect hard work and dignity of labour while expecting them to harvest where they have not sowed. Princes now eat in the morning because they are expecting to get something for nothing. These youths eat in the morning and just want to lie in their beds, not working, not doing anything, yet reaping off their friends, relatives and colleagues through their 360 percent a year returns. This is the reason why they have already lost. They will reap sooner or later sorrows and losses.

The only way for Nigeria to avoid the impending collision with these consequences of lack of virtues is to begin to raise an alarm right now. We need to begin to give our young people a clear message that only hard work can lead to true financial freedom. If we as a nation are to avoid the woes, curses and tragedies that come with laziness, we must take charge of giving sound orientation to our youths and future leaders by encouraging everyone to become workaholics.

As evil as Ponzi schemes and pyramids are, it would be wrong to put all the blames on them for our national decay and corruption. They only reveal who we are. What such schemes have revealed about the Nigerian population is that we are a nation void of the true understanding of hard work and the requirement for financial freedom. We have been deprived of true virtues and handed religion. We have become a nation famous for our religiosity without virtues.

Is religion really possible without virtues? I think this is the description of paganism, Religious but devoid of character and virtues. We must retrace our steps. The task of saving our nation from the painful repercussions of laziness has to be undertaken not just by the government, but by the religious leaders and the elite Nigerians. Such GET RICH QUICK schemes have only come to uncover our nakedness. We have been naked for a long time before they came. It is high time for us to use this opportunity to revisit our virtues as a nation. We must elevate hard work and make it a national theme.

Our pulpit must stop talking about miracles and breakthroughs because the message our youth are hearing is that through miracles and breakthroughs, you can get something out of nothing. What they are hearing is that it is possible to reap where you have not sowed. The national psyche of Nigerians today is more like "if it is good for me now, it doesn't matter what happens later."

If truth be told, our churches have largely contributed to this. Our messages of instant gratification have led to a whole generation of people who only want to see instant results, immediate relief and a painless profit. This is not the natural course of nature. For our youth to change, our messages must change. For our nation to change, our pulpit must change. We must begin to deliver relevant messages which are capable of building a healthy nation and future. Instead of messages that are only promising blessings, miracles, breakthroughs and wonders. We must replace these messages with preaching on virtues such as hard work, creativity, dedication, commitment, perseverance, diligence, responsibility, etc. We must teach people to become allergic to laziness. We must raise up workaholics who will work hard to better their lives and the nation at large. Make up your mind to urgently become a workaholic. Become allergic to laziness and join the train of those who will transform our nation via hard work, commitment and personal responsibility.

Dear friends, I do hope you learnt something from this chapter and have come to realise that all that maybe be needed to transform our nation and save it from recession is to introduce the message of the dignity of labour. We must change the get rich quick mentality of our youths and replace it with the mind set of work. Do not forget that if you want to subdue your promised land, you must become allergic to laziness and urgently become a workaholic. Finally, to prevent your life and that of your nation from decay, you and I must urgently become workaholics.

In the next chapter, I am going to be revealing to you the benefits of hard work and how you can turn your life around positively through it. I implore you to proceed with me as I share with you the examples of people who became great thanks to hard work.

NUGGETS FROM
CHAPTER THREE

1. The number one reason for recession in any nation is laziness. By that I mean the refusal of the citizens of that nation to become workaholics.

2. Any slothful society will come to decay sooner or later. In one way or the other, decay will come to the economy, systems, lifestyle, ministries, agencies, institutions and everything else.

3. Laziness brings decay, corruption and bad economy.

4. There is going to be brain drain, economic drain and all kinds of drainage will be going on in the society or country where there is a culture of laziness.

5. For any country to develop, it has to first of all overcome the culture of laziness in its citizens by teaching them to become workaholics.

6. Our people must once again realize that it is only hard work and excellence that leads to wealth creation.

7. It must once again become a common knowledge to our people that it is only the wealth that we create that we can share.

8. Every major outward change must first begin

in the mind. So for us to expect development in our nations, we must first bring development to the minds and understandings of our people.

9. One destructive mind-set that must be altered in our society is the thought that work is a curse.

10. Our government, media houses, schools, must focus on creating a new culture in our society. A culture of work. A culture of labour. A culture of diligence. A culture of hard work. A culture of perseverance. A culture of persistence. A culture of dignity of labour.

PRINCIPLES FROM
CHAPTER THREE

1. Until we teach our people to become
    workaholics, we cannot bring an end to
    the recession and national challenges
    that have plagued us as a nation

2. If our nation must become a developed
    nation, we must all become allergic to
    laziness. Until you and I become allergic to
    laziness, we cannot become workaholics

3. People who are workaholics are allergic to
    laziness. They cannot stand laziness because
    they hate it with a passion. Workaholics
    have a strong dislike for laziness.

4. Your life will be overgrown with thorns if
    you refuse to become a workaholic. Your
    life will be broken in pieces if you are not
    allergic to laziness. Laziness will destroy
    your life and endanger your future.

5. Anyone who does not work disgraces
    himself and steals from the wealth of those
    who do labour. If a man does not work,
    he gives nothing of value to the world.

6. We need to begin to give our young people
    a clear message that only hard work

can lead to true financial freedom.

6. We need to begin to give our young people a clear message that only hard work can lead to true financial freedom.

7. If we as a nation are to avoid the woes, curses and tragedies that come with laziness, we must take charge of giving sound orientation to our youths and future leaders by encouraging everyone to become workaholics.

8. The task of saving our nation from the painful repercussions of laziness has to be undertaken not just by the government, but by the religious leaders and the elite Nigerians.

9. Instead of messages that are only promising blessings, miracles, breakthroughs and wonders. We must replace these messages with preaching on virtues such as hard work, creativity, dedication, commitment, perseverance, diligence, responsibility, etc.

10. Become allergic to laziness and join the train of those who will transform our nation via hard work commitment and personal responsibility.

CHAPTER 4

THE BENEFITS OF HARD WORK

I am delighted to welcome you to this chapter of this book. That you have read up till this point is an indication that you truly want to become a workaholic. Having said in the last chapter that nations go into recession because of the refusal of its citizens to work hard, and that your life will decay if you decide to live a life of laziness, I will be glad to share with you in this chapter the benefits of hard work to nations and to individuals. I will be sharing with you the story of people who became great through hard work and how you too can become great and benefit from hard work.

MICHAEL JORDAN: AN EXAMPLE OF HARD WORK

Michael Jordan is one of the greatest ever examples of hard work and ambition beating out natural talent.

Michael Jordan was born on February 17, 1963, in Brooklyn, New York, one of James and Deloris Jordan's five children. The family moved to Wilmington, North Carolina, when Michael was very young. His father worked as a General Electric plant supervisor, and his mother worked at a bank. His father taught him to work hard and not to be tempted by street life. His mother taught him to sew, clean, and do laundry. Jordan loved sports but failed to make his high school basketball team as a sophomore. He continued to practice and made the team the next year. After high school he accepted a basketball scholarship to the University of North Carolina, where he played under head coach Dean Smith.

In Jordan's first season at North Carolina he was named Atlantic Coast Conference (ACC) Rookie of the Year for 1982. The team won the ACC championship, and Jordan made the clutch jump shot that beat Georgetown University for the championship of the National Collegiate Athletic Association (NCAA). Jordan led the ACC in scoring as a sophomore and as a junior. The Sporting News named him college player of the year for both years. He left North Carolina after his junior year and was selected by the Chicago Bulls of the National Basketball Association (NBA) as the third pick of the 1984 draft. Before joining the Bulls, Jordan was a member of the summer 1984 United States Olympic basketball team that won the gold medal in Los Angeles, California.

When Jordan was drafted by the Chicago Bulls they were a losing team, drawing only around six thousand fans to home games. Jordan quickly turned that around. His style of play and fierce spirit of competition reminded sportswriters and fans of Julius Erving who had been a superstar player during the 1970s. Jordan's incredible leaping ability and hang time thrilled fans in arenas around the league. In his first season he was named to the All-Star team and was later honoured as the league's Rookie of the Year.

Dear friends, what do you think made Michael Jordan so good that even his team mates admired him? The reason is simply because he was a workaholic. Workaholics are always without equals in whatever they do. They stand out and take the place of honour above all else. If you want to be as good as Michael Jordan in your own area of calling, then you have to be willing to go the extra mile of working harder than everyone else. You have to be willing to do whatever it takes to get to the top. Forget about what everyone else on the team is doing! If they're going at half speed, you go on full speed. They're just like everyone else out there. If you really want to stand out, then you must stand out in your hard work. You must become a workaholic. You have to be willing to step outside of your comfort zone. When others are satisfied with mediocrity and average, you should be uncomfortable with it. The reason why Michael Jordan had so much excellence in his career is because he is more committed and hardworking than everyone else. He is not satisfied with average and knows how to push himself above average. To truly excel in life, you must learn to push yourself above average by becoming a workaholic.

Average is the enemy of excellence, and average commitment will prevent you from enduring to the end.

KEVIN PEARSON

A broken foot side-lined Jordan for 64 games during the 1985–86 season, but he returned to score 49 points against the Boston Celtics in the first game of the playoffs and 63 in the second game—an NBA playoff record. The 1986–87 season was again one of individual successes, and Jordan started in the All-Star game after receiving a record 1.5 million votes. He became the first player since Wilt Chamberlain (1936–1999) to score 3,000 points in a single season. Jordan enjoyed personal success, but Chicago did not advance beyond the first round of the playoffs until 1988. Jordan concentrated on improving his other basketball skills, and in 1988 he was named Defensive Player of the Year. He was also named the league's Most Valuable Player (MVP) and became the first player to lead the league in both scoring and steals. He was again named MVP in that year's All-Star game.

In 1993, after a tough playoff series with the New York Knicks, the Bulls met the Phoenix Suns for the NBA championship. When it was over, Jordan was again playoff MVP, and Chicago had won a third straight title. That summer Jordan's father, James, was murdered by two men during a robbery attempt. Jordan was grief stricken, and his father's death, combined with media reports about his gambling, led him to announce his retirement from professional basketball in October. Jordan had won three straight NBA titles, three regular season MVP awards, three playoff MVP titles, seven consecutive scoring titles, and he was a member of the All-Star team every year that he was in the league. In just nine seasons he had become the Bulls all-time leading scorer.

RETURN TO GLORY

When Jordan returned to the Chicago Bulls during the 1994–95 regular season, people wondered, «Could he do it again?» After a summer of playing basketball during breaks from filming the live-action cartoon movie Space Jam, Jordan returned with a fierce determination to prove that he had the ability to get back on top. The 1995–96 Bulls finished the regular season 72–10, an NBA record for most wins in a season, and Jordan, with his shooting rhythm back, earned his eighth scoring title. He also became the tenth NBA player to score 25,000 career points and second fastest after Chamberlain to reach that mark. The Bulls went on to win their fourth NBA championship, overpowering the Seattle Supersonics in six games.

The defending champions had a tougher time during the 1996–97 season but entered the playoffs as expected. Sheer determination took the Bulls to their fifth NBA championship. Illness, injury, and at times a lack of concentration hurt the team. In the fifth game of the finals Jordan carried the team to victory despite suffering from a stomach virus. In the 1997–98 season the Bulls were again in the playoffs, and again they faced tough competition. As before, they were able to clinch the NBA championship, and Jordan claimed his sixth NBA finals MVP award.

HIS SECRET OF SUCCESS: HARD WORK

Dear friends, if you paid keen attention to the success story of Michael Jordan, you would have seen that Jordan was the force behind all the victories his team had. He could be regarded as a genius and the sole mastermind of the Chicago bull's success. The question therefore is, how did he become so good that he influenced the success of his team? What was the secret behind his skills and prowess in the game of basketball?

The answer to these questions is that Michael Jordan had prodigious physical gifts. But as his long-time coach Phil Jackson writes, it was hard work that made him a legend.

When Jordan first entered the league, his jump shot wasn't good enough. He spent his off season taking hundreds of jumpers a day until it was perfect. In a piece at NBA.com, Jackson writes that Jordan's defining characteristic wasn't his talent, but having the humility to know he had to work constantly to be the best.

Dear friends, I want you to take note of a fact from what you just read; and the fact is that Jordan spent his off season taking hundred jumpers a day until it was perfect. That was hard work at its best. When his colleagues would while away their off seasons doing nothing to improve their skills, Jordan was becoming a workaholic by constantly training, taking hundred jumpers per day. It was not his talent that made him exceptional but his hard work. It was only thanks to his hard work that he became better than his colleagues and stood as the best basketball player in the world. It may be tiring to take hundred jumpers per day but Jordan would not give up. He would persist till the end. That is a virtue that is common to all great people, they know how to persevere and persist on hard work. He became great thanks to determination and persistence.

"Nothing in this world can take the place of persistence. Talent will not: nothing is more common than unsuccessful men with talent. Genius will not; unrewarded genius is almost a proverb. Education will not: the world is full of educated derelicts. Persistence and determination alone are omnipotent."

CALVIN COOLIDGE

Jordan's other professional life as a businessman was never off track. Profitable endorsements (ads in which he voiced his support for certain products) for companies such as Nike and Wheaties, as well as his own golf company and products such as Michael Jordan cologne (which reportedly sold 1.5 million bottles in its first two months), made Jordan a multimillionaire. In 1997 he was ranked the world's highest paid athlete, with a $30 million contract—the largest one-year salary in sports history—and approximately $40 million a year in endorsement fees.

Jordan retired for a second time in 1999, ending his career on a high note just after the official end of a labour dispute between NBA players and team owners. Many people saw him as the greatest basketball player ever, and his retirement was called the end of an era. In 2000 Jordan became part-owner and president of basketball operations of the Washington Wizards. This made him only the third African American owner in the NBA. He also gained an ownership stake in the Washington Capitals hockey team. Also in 2000, Jordan celebrated the first year of his $1 million grant program to help teachers make a difference in their schools.

Dear friends, the success story of Michael Jordan is one that many people desire to become their own story. His excellence is unparalleled but that was because he decided to become a workaholic. He had fame, money and an excellent career which is the kind of life that everyone desires. However, we must all learn to admire his hard work too if we really want to become successful as he was. Below are a few comments about the legend Michael Jordan:

As a phenomenal athlete with a unique combination of fundamental soundness, grace, speed, power, artistry, improvisational ability and an unquenchable competitive desire, Jordan single-handedly redefined the NBA superstar.

Even contemporaneous superstars recognized the unparalleled position of Jordan. Magic Johnson said" There's Michael Jordan and there is the rest of us" Larry Bird, following a playoff game where Jordan dropped 63 points on the Boston Celtics in just his second season, appraisal of the young player was "God disguised as Michael Jordan"

Dear friends, as I summarise the success story of the legend Michael Jordan, I want us to see a list of qualities that defined the genius.

- He was Hard working
- He was a workaholic
- He was determined to be the best
- He was persistent
- He endured hard training sessions.
- He was committed to his goals
- He trained harder than everyone else
- He made himself competitive
- He made himself the greatest basketball player ever
- He was an investor and a philanthropist

He became great thanks to those qualities. My advice to you is that you emulate him by bringing those qualities into your life too irrespective of what your career is. Finally, I would like to say that if you must become the best in whatever you do, you must urgently become a workaholic like Michael Jordan was. There is no greatness without hard work. No one has gotten to the top without first becoming a workaholic. That is why I urge you to urgently become a workaholic if you desire greatness and success in life.

> *"I do not know anyone who has got to the top without hard work. That is the recipe. It will not always get you to the top, but should get you pretty near"*
>
> ## MARGARET THATCHER

PERSONAL BENEFITS OF HAVING THE RIGHT ATTITUDE TO WORK

In this session, I want to quickly outline the benefits that right attitude to work would bring to our people and nations. People must be taught that money is not the most important benefit of work. Work indeed has many more benefits than money as I have stated below:

- We work to firstly realize our hidden potentials. Work therefore is the paramount key to discovering yourself. God has hidden in each and every one of us so many abilities, gifts and resources that could only be activated by work.

- We work to discover and release the potential of the earth around us. God in his infinite wisdom has deposited in everything potential for growth and multiplication. There is worth everywhere and in everything we see. Work therefore is designed to release all this abundance of wealth hidden inside everything. For example, it is only by work we extract gold from the soil. It takes work to discover the oil that is already deposited in the ground. It is work that turns a hill of coal into carats of diamond.

- Work is given to us by God as an instrument to multiply resources. Everything God created was created in a seed form, small and miniature. It takes work to increase and multiply every resource we see around us.

- Work is the divine provision God has given to every man through which we can all provide for our needs, for the needs of our families and for others.

"He who tills his land will have plenty of bread, but he who follows frivolity will have poverty enough."

PROVERBS 28:19

- Work gives us access and opportunities. Our young men and women must be taught that through hard work, they can create opportunities for themselves and others.

- God told us to be fruitful, multiply and subdue the earth. The only instrument that is given to all men equally to do this is work.

- God only gives men power to make wealth, meaning God does not give wealth, he gives the power to work for it. (Deut. 8:18)

- Through work, we serve, minister, and become God's stewards on the earth.

- All forms of works bring profit. Meaning that true work will facilitate the development and advancement of any nation or people. Work must not just be physical, we must teach our people that work is both mental, spiritual and physical.

"In all labour there is profit, but idle chatter leads only to poverty."

PROVERBS 14:24

NATIONAL BENEFITS OF HAVING THE RIGHT ATTITUDE TO WORK

Friends, the benefits of hard work are not just for individuals but for nations as well. God gave us the grace and ability to work, because it is only through work we can resolve national issues. Just as hard work could make an individual great, so it is with nations. A nation can be made great just by teaching its citizens the principles and benefits of hard work. That is why it is my belief that if our governments in Africa take this message seriously, we could actually end up building our own nations to become developed and advanced just like any other country in the first world. If we could introduce the culture of DIGNITY OF LABOR to our societies, our young people will no longer keep on risking their precious lives in the Mediterranean ocean, in an attempt to find a better life in the so called developed countries. If we teach our citizens to become workaholics, they would all excel and become kings and sons of nobles.

> *"Do you see a man who excels in his work? He will stand before kings; He will not stand before unknown men."*
>
> PROVERBS 22:29

Whatever any nation has done, could be easily replicated if we know the principles and the secrets behind it. That is why I have decided to share this principle of hard work and dignity of labour with my nation Nigeria, countries in Africa and other developing nations of the world.

If Nigeria and Africa, Mexico and Latin America, other developing countries are to stop losing their best sons to the disaster of tragic deaths in places like the Mediterranean ocean and the Gulf of Mexico, then we must take this message seriously. It is my prayers that the governments of these countries would take a serious look at this topic and implement the principle so as to lead their nations to growth and economic prosperity.

THE DECEPTION OF RETIREMENT

In America, some businessmen who want to sell their books have come up with interesting stories about what age to retire. For example, retirement at age 25, 30, 35etc. This is not natural. It is rather natural to work and work hard because if it were not so, God wouldn't have told Adam to work. Retirement is the desire of an indolent man. Workaholics do not desire retirement because they cannot survive without work. I know this may sound crazy to a lot of people to say that retirement is a lazy man's desire. But I know what I am talking about and I believe all workaholics understand this too.

The modern model for retirement was created by Otto von Bismarck, chancellor of Germany, in 1883. He announced that the state would pay a pension to any non-working citizen older than 65, setting in place an arbitrary retirement age that still exists to this day. Retirement is therefore man's idea not God's. If you think I'm out of my mind, perhaps the facts below could help buttress the points I have been trying to make in this book.

Retirement isn't a natural state for human beings. Humans are created to work and by that work sustain their lives.

Studies suggest that death comes sooner to those who retire.

One study, which followed the lives of former Shell Oil workers for 20 years, concluded that those who retired early had a significantly higher mortality rate than those who continued to work.

A similar study tracking the lives of more than 16,000 Greek citizens found that retirees were 51 percent more likely to die than those of the same age who continued to work. The link between retirement and early death may have to do with a decrease in activity -- as most retirees live a more sedentary life once they no longer work -- that can lead to increased health problems.

You will not be able to survive on pension. You will always run out of money.

You are going to be bored if you stop working.

Life is always without meaning if we stop working. Work gives purpose to life and without work, depression and boredom become consistent in our lives.

Finally, I want to state that retirement is only the beginning not the end. Most people think that retirement is the end of work. I however want to say that it is the end to a new beginning. If you are working for the government or for a boss, you may only retire because you need time to begin to work for yourself. You can stop working for salary and start working for yourself. Therefore do not be deceived into thinking that retirement is the end of work. It is not. It is only the beginning of a new kind of work.

Dear friends, I believe by now you will agree with me that we were created to work. The natural order of things for man is that he must work to sustain his life. You will be going against the law of nature if you refuse to work and hurriedly retire. Even God himself worked and he is still working. You can even say it to a large extent that God is a Workaholic because Jesus said that hitherto my father works and so I must work" What he was saying is that God who is the eternal creator has never stopped working. He works continuously. Why does he keep working? He works because it is his nature to work. It is that same image and likeness of God that you and I possess. Hence we cannot but exercise that nature of work and become workaholics. God who is the creator of heaven and earth, has everything and doesn't need anything, doesn't work to get salary, an apartment etc. works because that is His nature. If you will not emulate the hard working character of the great names I have mentioned in this book, you at least have God himself as an example of a workaholic to emulate. Whether you like it or not you must urgently become a workaholic or be ready to face the consequences.

As I bring this chapter to a close, I want to believe that now you know the benefits of hard work and that it is beyond just having money. You would have seen from this chapter that hard work is beneficial to individuals as well as to nations. I also will be glad if you took note of the fact that retirement is not the natural order of things for man but work. When man retires and stops working, he puts his life on a quick journey to death.

In the next chapter, I am going to be showing you how it is better to be hard working than to be talented. I am sure you don't want to deprive yourself of that revelation. Come on lets proceed to the next chapter to see for yourself how hard work beats talent if talent doesn't work hard.

NUGGETS FROM CHAPTER FOUR

1. Workaholics are always without equals in whatever they do. They stand out and take the place of honour above all else.

2. If you really want to stand out, then you must stand out in your hard work. You must become a workaholic.

3. When others are satisfied with mediocrity and average, you should be uncomfortable with it.

4. To truly excel in life, you must learn to push yourself above average by becoming a workaholic.

5. That is a virtue that is common to all great people, they know how to persevere and persist on hard work.

6. If you must become the best in whatever you do, you must urgently become a workaholic.

7. There is no greatness without hard work. No one has gotten to the top without first becoming a workaholic.

8. We work to firstly realize our hidden potentials. Work therefore is the paramount key to discovering yourself.

9. We work to discover and release the

potential of the earth around us.

10. It takes work to increase and multiply

every resource we see around us.

PRINCIPLES FROM
CHAPTER FOUR

1. Through work, we serve, minister, and become God's stewards on the earth.

2. A nation can be made great just by teaching its citizens the principles and benefits of hard work.

3. If we teach our citizens to become workaholics, they would all excel and become kings and sons of nobles

4. The natural order of things for man is that he must work to sustain his life.

5. You will be going against the law of nature if you refuse to work and hurriedly retire.

6. Whether you like it or not you must urgently become a workaholic or be ready to face the consequences.

7. You are more likely to find yourself unsatisfied with your retirement years, both financially and emotionally, if you don't have some

CHAPTER 5

TALENT IS NOT ENOUGH, HARD WORK MAKES THE DIFFERENCE

I n this chapter, I am going to be showing you how hard work and not talent determines greatness. Example of great names like Usain Bolt will be used to better explain my points. I implore you to read on as this chapter may be the turning point of your life.

> *"Talent is cheaper than table salt. What separates the talented individual from the successful one is a lot of hard work"*
> STEPHEN KING

Dear friends, do you know any very talented individual who is not yet great or famous? Just look around your church, school or environment. Can you find anyone who you believe to be talented and yet is not well known on a world stage? Well if your answer is yes, then you are not alone. I too have seen a lot of talented people who are just local champions. I know a lot of talented people who are still living in poverty and absolute lack of financial freedom. In fact I have come to the conclusion that there are more talented people who are living in mediocrity than there are who are living in excellence and financial wealth. The reason for such tragedy is not far -fetched. The first inference that one could draw from the foregoing is the fact that talent is not enough, hard work is what makes the difference. Not all successful people are talented and not all talented people are successful. However the few talented people who have become successful in life have only become successful because they worked hard to improve their talent. They refined their talent through hard work and thanks to that, they became more successful than their counterparts who only had talent but lacked hard work, those who are too lazy to refine their talent. To excel more than anyone else in life you must learn to refine your talents through hard work.

REFINING YOUR DIAMOND THROUGH HARD WORK

Your talents and gifts are like diamond. If you don't refine them through hard work, they can never appreciate in value. The first thing you need to do to succeed in life is to discover your talents and gifting. The second thing you should have in place to be able to rank among the great names in history is to make sure that you don't leave your talents and gifts in a raw state. Your talent is just like diamond. Let's assume your talent is in the area of music. Don't just be satisfied with the fact that you can play the keyboard or sing and then just leave your talent at that state. You are not the only one who is talented with the gift of singing. The idea of this book is to challenge you to being the best in whatever you do. My sincere desire is that you rise from the complacency of just having a talent to becoming the best in the world in the area of your gifting and talents. That is however only possible through hard work. For you to become the best in the world you must become a workaholic and make yourself competitive. Even if someone is more talented than you, with hard work you can become better than that person if he or she refuses to work hard.

"There may be people who have more talent than you, but there's no excuse for anyone to work harder than you do - and I believe that."

DEREK JETER

You have no control over what talent you are born with or who is born with more talent than you but you have total control over how diligent you could become. Diligence is what makes the difference. You will never be able to become competitive if you leave your talents and gifts in the raw state. You won't be able to compete at a world level and become the best if you don't work hard to cultivate your talents. You will never be able to add value to the world. So after you discover your talent, the next thing you should do is to refine it. In Africa for example, some village people go about looking for diamond and after finding the raw diamond, they sell it out at a very cheap price. Why do they sell it at a very cheap price? The reason is because raw diamond is not expensive. The diamond that is very expensive is the refined diamond. Why are they very expensive? It is because they are polished, cleaned and well refined through the process of work. Any gift and calling that is refined will automatically increase in value and in worth. Therefore you have to put a system in place for polishing your gift. That system that is needed to polish your gift better than anyone else is called hard work. The difference between talented people is hard work. Anybody who works hardest to develop his talents becomes king over the others. Do not make the mistake of thinking that you can become great just because you are endowed with talent, no sir! There are a bunch of talented people roaming the streets and struggling to survive in a world where workaholics become kings. You will remain a servant if you don't become diligent in developing your talent. You have to improve and refine your gifts. Just being good in music is not a guarantee that you will be competitive and it is also not a guarantee that you can earn a living from it. Most people write to me asking about how they can make money from their gifts. The answer I give to them is that, even if you know your gifts and calling, until you polish and refine it you can never make money from it. Until you invest in your gift and add value to it, it will never become valuable. If you don't improve, refine and polish your gift, it will never be able to reward you. That is why you see so many talented and gifted people who cannot make ends meet. An indolent man who is highly talented will always depend on and beg from a workaholic who is not as talented for survival. Your gift will only be able to feed you if you refine and add value to it. How do you refine your gift, for example if you are called into music? You must invest time and energy rehearsing again and again. You must attend music classes to perfect your skills either in vocals or in instrumentals. You will have to work hard by dedicating ten thousand hours of rehearsals and practice into refining that gift if you want to be one of the best musicians in the world. This is called the rule of 10,000 hours which was proposed by Malcolm Gladwell. This rule states that 10,000 hours of "deliberate practice" are needed to become world-class in any field. Therefore, you must invest ten thousand hours into perfecting your skills. You will have to work harder by investing more time into the development of your talents than every other person. That was why Michael Jordan stood out and became exceptional in his career. He worked harder than everyone else in refining and perfecting his gifts and talents. Don't forget. Talent is not enough! Talent must be polished and refined. Value must be added to your talent. You must improve your skills but that is going to be possible only through hard work.

Now the question in your mind may be "why must I work hard to improve and refine my gift? Can't I still fulfil my purpose without refining it?" Well! You can still fulfil your purpose without refining your gifts but you will only be able to do that at a lower level. You will only end up as a local champion if you don't work hard to refine your gifts. You can't feed from your gift if you don't invest hard work into it. You will be as cheap as the raw diamond if you don't refine your gifts. For your talent to be able to sustain you, you must work hard to improve on it. Only refined diamond costs a fortune.

WORK HARD ON YOUR TALENTS AND YOU WON'T NEED A MIRACLE

Jamaican Usain Bolt is an Olympic legend who has been called "the fastest man alive" for smashing world records and winning 9 gold medals as a reigning champion at the 2008, 2012 and 2016 Summer Games.

Usain Bolt was born in Jamaica on August 21, 1986. Both a standout cricket player and a sprinter early on, Bolt's natural speed was noticed by coaches at school, and he began to focus solely on sprinting under the tutelage of Pablo Mc-Neil, a former Olympic sprint athlete. (Glen Mills would later serve as Bolt's coach and mentor.) As early as age 14, Bolt was wowing fans of sprinting with his lightning speed, and he won his first high school championships medal in 2001, taking the silver in the 200-meter race.

At the age of 15, Bolt took his first shot at success on the world stage at the 2002 World Junior Championships in Kingston, Jamaica, where he won the 200-meter dash, making him the youngest world-junior gold medallist ever. Bolt's feats impressed the athletics world, and he received the International Association of Athletics Foundation's Rising Star Award that year and soon was given the apt nickname "Lightning Bolt."

Bolt reached the world Top 5 rankings in 2005 and 2006. In 2007, Bolt broke the national 200-meter record held for over 30 years by Donald Quarrie, and earned two silver medals at the World Championship in Osaka, Japan. These medals boosted Bolt's desire to run, and he took a more serious stance toward his career.

Bolt announced that he would run the 100-meter and 200-meter events at the Beijing Summer Olympics. In the 100-meter final, Bolt broke the world record, winning in 9.69 seconds. Not only was the record set without a favourable wind, but he also visibly slowed down to celebrate before he finished. He went on to win three gold medals and break three world records in Beijing.

At the 2012 Summer Olympic Games, held in London, Bolt won his fourth Olympic gold medal in the men's 100-meter race, beating rival Yohan Blake, who won silver in the event. Bolt ran the race in 9.63 seconds, a new Olympic record. The win marked Bolt's second consecutive gold medal in the 100-meter event. He went on to compete in the men's 200, claiming his second consecutive gold medal in that race. He is the first man to win both the 100 and 200 in consecutive Olympic Games, as well as the first man to ever win back-to-back gold medals in double sprints. Bolt's accomplishments have made him the first man in history to set three world records in a single Olympic Games competition.

Hold on a little friends, let's pause the story for a while and discuss the possibility of such feats as was displayed by Usain Bolt. Usain bolt is a record breaker and a limit setter. He has broken Olympic records and set new ones. No man had won back-to-back gold medals in double sprints but Bolt did. No man had set three world records in a single Olympic games, but Bolt did. Never before in history has any man won both the 100m and 200m in a consecutive Olympic game but Bolt did. Why did he set all these new world records? Were there no other talented athletes at the Olympics? Well, I guess you know the answer. Almost everyone who comes to represent their countries in an Olympic game is talented and to some extent are hard workers. But you know what! The workaholic takes it all. He takes all the gold medals. He breaks all the old records and sets up new records. The workaholic is the king of the games. He rules over the hard workers and the slothful. Such is the man Usain bolt. The workaholic is the one qualified to be crowned the fastest man on earth. It is not talent that made Usain bolt the king, hard work did.

Bolt returned to Olympic glory at the 2016 Summer Olympic Games when he won gold in the 100-meter race, making him the first athlete to win three successive titles in the event. He finished the race in 9.81 seconds with American runner and rival Justin Gatlin who took silver, 0.08 seconds behind him.

The workaholic is not only proud of himself but also sure of himself. When you become a workaholic you can predict the outcome of the game even before it begins. Listen to what Bolt, the workaholic had to say about himself:

"This is why I came here, to the Olympics, to prove to the world that I'm the best — again," he told reporters at a news conference. "It always feels good to go out on top, you know what I mean?"

He continued his winning streak, taking gold in the 200-meter in 19.78 seconds. "What else can I do to prove I am the greatest?" Bolt said in an interview with BBC Sports. " I'm trying to be one of the greatest, to be among Muhammad Ali and Pele.

I have made the sport exciting, I have made people want to see the sport. I have put the sport on a different level."

Dear friends, if you are not challenged by the statements above, I doubt if anything else could challenge you. Usain bolt could talk that way because he knows how much hard work he has invested into perfecting and refining his talent. You can become that assured of victories in life if you could become a workaholic. It doesn't matter what career you are practising, if you could just become a workaholic, you will be so certain of your greatness that the world will celebrate you for it.

The "fastest man alive" remained undefeated in what he said would be the last race of his Olympic career, the 4x100-meter relay which he ran with teammates Asafa

Powell, Yohan Blake and Nickel Ashmeade. Anchoring the race, Bolt led the Jamaican team to win gold, crossing the finish line in 37.27. Japan won silver and Canada took the bronze. It was the third consecutive gold medal win for Bolt in Rio, and the completion of a "triple-triple" with a total of 9 gold medals earned over the course of his Olympic career. Bolt joins Paavo Nurmi of Finland (in 1920, 1924 and 1928) and Carl Lewis of the United States (in 1984, 1988, 1992 and 1996) who have won the most career gold medals at the Olympics.

If you work hard to polish, refine and add value to your gift, that same gift will begin to add value to you for the rest of your life.

GOD DOESN'T RUN AN OLYMPIC RACE

My country Nigeria is full of people who out of laziness expect God to do for them what they should do for themselves. Laziness has so eaten deep into the fabrics of our nation that everybody now begins to ask God to come do what hard work could do for them. God has blessed every nation with a gift called work and any man who applies the gift of hard work does not need to beg God for success in life. Unfortunately for us, we have rejected hard work and are depending on God for everything even to win an Olympic race. For example in the 2016 Olympic games, all my country men were so happy when they saw a Nigerian athlete who ran in the same heat with Usain Bolt, the fastest man in the world. The Nigerian athlete happened to run his personal best and became number two after Usain Bolt but that was just the preliminary race. It was just the heat and if you know about athletics you will bear witness that the heat is nothing compared to the main race itself.

In the semi-finals of the race, the Nigerian guy was in the race again with Usain Bolt but that was when Usain bolt started running properly and putting energy in his race. Guess what happened to the Nigerian guy. Of course he became last and all the Nigerians became quiet after that.

Why did he become last in the race? I will tell you why. He became last because he thought God runs Olympic race. He failed because he thought God decides who wins an Olympic race. Little did he know that it is hard work that decides who becomes the winner in any race of life. How did I know he was depending on God to run the race for him?

I listened to the interview of the Nigerian guy before he went for the Olympics and the journalists asked him how he was going to win the games considering that he had not really prepared himself via hard work and consistent practices. He was asked how he taught he could perform at the games knowing that he was going to compete with Usain Bolt, the world number one athlete and with other competent athletes from different countries. You know what his response was? He said "Oh yea, if Usain Bolt can do it I can do it also. He is a man, I am a man too. God has given me two legs as he gave to Bolt and I believe by the grace of God I can do it. I believe God will do it. God can do anything. Anything could happen"

What a response! I was amazed by his religious response and at that point I just got ashamed of my country and I said "this country is totally hopeless. How can you just be thinking that because God gave you two legs and gave Usain Bolt two legs that you are going to be competitive? How on earth could you be thinking that God would do it? How could you just be dependent on miracles to win an Olympic race? If he had known that God doesn't run an Olympic race, he probably would not have depended on God for his success. If he had known that it takes diligence to win the race he would have urgently become a workaholic. In an attempt to show everyone that God doesn't run nor decides who wins an Olympic race I did something.

After listening to his religious ranting in that interview, I went and looked for a video clip of Usain Bolt training sessions and put it on my blog so that Nigerians would see it. I wanted him and my country-men to know that Usain Bolt was not going to win the race because God gave him two legs. I wanted to show them that even though all the competing athletes had two legs, only those who worked hardest to refine their gifts will become top of the list of champions. I was trying to tell my fellow citizens that you cannot win an Olympic race because you are prayerful. It doesn't matter how many times you fast and pray, it will not make you an Olympic champion. People don't become Olympic champions by prayers but by hard work. It doesn't matter how much you believe in God, if you will not become diligent in adding value to your gifts and refining your talents, you can never become the world best in your area of gifting.

It is true that God gives gifts to men but men must work on, improve and refine their gifts if they must become great through their gifts. It's nice to be talented, but the old saying is true:

"Hard work beats talent when talent doesn't work hard."
TIM NOTKE

Even though God gave two legs to Usain Bolt and the Nigerian athlete, Bolt however was improving his gift by serious hard work. He was training tirelessly, building himself and adding value to his gift. He had the best doctors and best coaches. He had the best gym. He did all sorts of physical work-outs. He wasn't fasting and praying for a miracle to win the Olympic race. He was rather creating value in himself by relentless trainings and hard work.

He spends his time refining his gift and thanks to that he is world fastest man. Through hard work, he continuously refines his running skills and that has put his name on the pages of history. Usain Bolt didn't need a miracle to win the race. He is world fastest man not because he believed in miracles. It was not God who made him win the race by miracles. No! He simply won because he constantly refines his skills through hard work.

While Nigerian athletes and journalists were busy discussing how God would help Nigeria in the Olympic Games, Usain Bolt was busy investing in himself through hard work, polishing and refining his skills via rigorous trainings. He does all kinds of physical workouts on a daily basis. Instead of severe trainings, our athletes would rather depend on God to help them win. No wonder my country could not boast of a single gold in the 2016 Olympic Games. The reason is because we had no workaholics who had prepared themselves via hard work. Until you add value to yourself by refining your gift, you will never become competitive and you will keep hoping on miracles. Until you become a workaholic you will keep depending on God for everything. Unfortunately, God doesn't run an Olympic race.

MIRACLES ARE ONLY
SUPPLEMENTARY ON EARTH

If you've ever listened to Nigerian sport journalists and analysts before an Olympic game, you would probably have heard them talk about how Nigeria could win the gold medals through the help of God. The Nigerian sport journalists are always saying "Oh God will do it. We believe God will help our team. He did it the other time and he can do it again". They are using miracles as their only hope of winning an Olympic game as if miracle is the order of the day. No wonder we don't win medals. I am not surprised about how backward the whole country is. It is because Nigerians think that miracle is the way to succeeding in life. They believe that God would do everything for them. No matter what you talk to a Nigerian about, he will tell you "God will do it" Nigerians want God to do everything for them while they lazy about doing nothing.

This religious mind-set is what has hindered our country from progressive development. My country is backward because when men should be working and perfecting their God-given gifts and talent, they rather go to prayer meetings to ask God for miracles to succeed in life. This indolent religious mind-set is not only expressed in the world of sport but in almost every sector of our economy. The reason why things are not working in Nigeria is simply because men have relinquished their roles to God. While God expects them to work hard and succeed through the unique talents and natural resources he has blessed them with, they are rather begging God to come down and do their jobs for them. Nigerians are always expecting manna to fall from heaven. They are always looking forward to a miracle from God instead of working hard to better themselves and become competitive on the world stage. Life is not meant to be lived by miracles. When it comes to life on the earth, miracles are only supplementary. Miracle is only secondary, it is not the order of the day. We are not meant to be living on miracles. When it comes to life on the earth, miracles are only an exception. You should only pray for a miracle if what you are asking for is not a possibility with humans. But if it is what a man can do, then you don't need a miracle to get it done, you need hard work. If a man can do the job, then God should not be disturbed. You should only call on God after you have done all the hard work that could be done to succeed. However chances are that after enough hard work, you will rarely need a miracle to succeed in life.

When a legend like Usain bolt ran the 100 meters in 9.58 seconds in an ecstatic stadium atmosphere, did he attain that feat here and there in that stadium that day? When Michael Jordan won all six finals that he played in, do you think that was just a miracle that was following him all the days of his life, or did he get lucky? Was it because he was the most fervent prayer warrior in the world? The answer is No! It was diligence not prayers that made them succeed. All the men and women who have become great through hard work and constant refining of their gifts and talents, didn't need to bother God much for miracles, yet they succeeded in life. I therefore submit that begging God for a miracle is only a lazy man's approach to run away from his responsibilities.

Nigerians are always complaining, oh! God is not providing for me! God is not doing this! God is not doing that! Let me tell you something; God is not going to provide for you if you don't become a workaholic. If you don't work hard to refine and polish your gift and talent, there will be nothing God can do to help you. His greatest provision to you are the gifts and talents he has blessed you with. His best gifts to you are the time, life and work that he has given to you freely. Use these provisions to better your life and make yourself great. Stop accusing God for your failures and mediocrity. God is not to be blamed for your lack of progress and backwardness. If you want to increase your influence and become a household name on the earth, stop depending on miracles. Go and sharpen your gifts and talents. Urgently become a workaholic. Go and work hard on yourself and make yourself competitive and you will soon discover that hard work is the key to greatness.

> "...talent means nothing, while experience, acquired in humility and with hard work, means everything."
> PATRICK SÜSKIND

WORK HARD BEHIND THE SCENE! ENJOY ON THE WORLD STAGE

Most times when we see champions or people who are successful in life we only tend to envy them and desire to be like them. We don't find out how they were able to get to such a stage in their lives where success has become synonymous with their names. Every great person you see now once paid a price to become great. When you see and hear about the legends of sports like Michael Jordan, Carl Lewis, Usain Bolt, Tiger Woods, Serena Williams, Cristiano Ronaldo, Lionel Messi, Michael Schumacher, you will also discover that behind every one of these heroes that millions celebrate all over the world for their public performances and successes on the world stage, is a hidden private lifestyle and philosophy behind the scenes. These men and women on daily basis, pay a huge price privately to come to the lime light that the world sees. That price is the price of hard work. If we must admire their success, we must also admire the hard work that led to that success. That is the essence of this book. My intention is to teach you not to just admire the success of others but to admire the hard work behind the success. When you admire the hard work and practise it, you will soon become the next success story in the world. The hard work is usually behind the scenes, but the enjoyment is on the world stage. If you work hard behind the scenes, you will enjoy on the world stage.

> *"Majority of people don't see the amount of work and years ambitious people invest behind the scenes, but as soon as they succeed with their dreams, they would insinuate that they were lucky."*
> EDMOND MBIAKA

The quote above completely explains the state of most citizens in my country. They all think that it is by luck and miracles that people rise to prominence. They do not know how much work has been done behind the scenes. Instead of working behind the scene to become the best in their career, they just relax and expect luck to happen to them. Until you work hard on yourself to become a professional in what you do, you can never rise to the top. When we see legends like Usain Bolts, we are often tempted to think that they got to the height of their career by luck. Well, let me tell you what Usain Bolt said once. He said the Olympic race is just the enjoyment time for him and that the real work is in the training sessions. The major work is behind the scenes. He trained so hard once that he was vomiting during the training sessions and his dad was amazed to see how much hard work and suffering he goes through during his training session. His dad said he couldn't watch him go through such hard work. You see, that hard work is the secret of his achievements in the world of sports. The same hard work that you are running away from is the first requirement that you need to get to the world stage. If you keep running away from hard work you better be ready to also run away from greatness and stardom. Only those who work hard behind the scenes finally become announced to the public on the world stage. He is the greatest because he puts in the hard work that is needed and he is determined to win. If you want to be announced on the world stage, you better urgently become a workaholic.

Having read this chapter, I believe it is obvious to you now that talent is not enough and that hard work is what makes the difference. The central truth in this chapter was that without hard work, talent is almost useless and that the workaholic is superior to the talented man if he doesn't work hard. Therefore there is need for you to refine and polish your talents through hard work and you will become a champion in whatever you do.

In the next chapter, I want you to know that everyone is looking for a workaholic, the whole world is in need of workaholics and you could be the one they are looking for. Read on friends, let me show you what will happen to you if you decide to become a workaholic.

NUGGETS FROM
CHAPTER FIVE

1. In fact I have come to the conclusion that there are more talented people who are living in mediocrity than there are who are living in excellence and financial wealth.

2. Talent is not enough, hard work is what makes the difference. Not all successful people are talented and not all talented people are successful

3. The few talented people who have become successful in life have only become successful because they worked hard to improve their talent.

4. To excel more than anyone else in life you must learn to refine your talents through hard work

5. Your talents and gifts are like diamond. If you don't refine them through hard work, they can never appreciate in value

6. Your talents and gifts are like diamond. If you don't refine them through hard work, they can never appreciate in value. The first thing you need to do to succeed in life is to discover your talents and gifting. The second thing you should have in place to be able to rank among the great names in history is to make sure that you don't leave your talents and gifts in a raw state.

7. Anybody who works hardest to develop his talents becomes king over the others

8. There are a bunch of talented people roaming the streets and struggling to survive in a world where workaholics become kings.

9. You will remain a servant if you don't work hard to develop your talent. You have to improve and refine your gifts. Just being good in music is not a guarantee that you will be competitive and it is also not a guarantee that you can earn a living from it.

10. Until you invest in your gift and add value to it, it will never become valuable.

PRINCIPLES FROM
CHAPTER FIVE

1. If you don't improve, refine and polish your gift, it will never be able to reward you

2. A lazy man who is highly talented will always depend on and beg from a workaholic who is not as talented for survival.

3. You must invest ten thousand hours into perfecting your skills. You will have to work harder by investing more time into the development of your talents than every other person.

4. You must improve your skills but that is going to be possible only through hard work.

5. For your talent to be able to sustain you, you must work hard to improve on it. Only refined diamond costs a fortune.

6. The workaholic takes it all. He takes all the gold medals. He breaks all the old records and sets up new records. The workaholic is the king of the games.

7. It doesn't matter how much you believe in God, if you will not work hard to add value to your gifts and refine your gifts, you can never become the world best in your area of gifting.

8. Only those who work hard behind the scenes finally become announced to the public on the world stage. If you want to be announced on the world stage, you better urgently become a workaholic

9. Become a workaholic and you will rule your world. Remember, hard work beats talent if talent doesn't work hard.

10. Become a workaholic and you will rule your world. Remember, hard work beats talent if talent doesn't work hard.

IN SEARCH OF WORKAHOLICS. DO YOU KNOW ANY?

Dear friends, in the previous chapter, we discussed the importance of working hard to refine your talents and skills. We said that when you become a workaholic, you will be placed above your counterparts who are talented but are not workaholics. In this chapter, I will further explain why that is so and how everyone will demand your skills and talents if you become a workaholic. While everyone is in need of a workaholic, no one wants to associate with the lazy man or slothful person. Read on dear friends as I tell you why the workaholic is in high demand.

EVERYONE IS IN NEED OF WORKAHOLICS

The path of a lazy man or slothful person will be littered with sharp thorns as if they are walking bear footed on thorns or nails but the way of the diligent is a high way. That is to say that for a Workaholic doors open to him. Everybody is looking for a Workaholic who will sit down and do all the work and who will not leave until all the jobs are done. There is no employer that will say he doesn't need a Workaholic. That is why the life of a workaholic person is a high way. His life is always on the upward and forward and nothing stops him neither are thorns laid in his way. He enjoys a free and wonderful ride in his life. Everybody is looking for a workaholic. It doesn't matter the field of life, a workaholic is always on a high demand. Nobody wants a lazy man but everybody is ready to pay whatever it takes to get a workaholic. The reason is because, the workaholic gets the job done faster and better. A workaholic doesn't look for jobs, jobs look for him. Employers would retrench an indolent man just to get him replaced by a workaholic. If you don't become a workaholic, nobody will need you. The whole world is looking for a workaholic. The coaches in premiere and champions league are screaming "I need a workaholic do you know any?" The managers in Shell and NNPC are shouting" I need a workaholic do you know any?" The university management is screaming the same thing. Every area of life needs a workaholic. Will they find you? Can you be diligent enough to be recommended for the job?

Nigeria's unemployment rate rose for the seventh straight quarter to 13.9 percent in the third quarter of 2016 from 13.3 percent in the previous period. It was the highest level since 2009. Unemployment Rate in Nigeria averaged 9.52 percent from 2006 until 2016.

With such a high rate of unemployment, one is left to imagine what will happen to the future of our nation. Millions of people roam the streets unemployed. Others have resorted to sleeping, eating and watching movies. Amidst the state of unemployment, the workaholic still gets employed. A man who is a workaholic is being sorted for in high demand. If there are no jobs and spaces are limited, the workaholic is given preference and employed first. Such a high level of competition for limited job spaces should challenge you to urgently become a workaholic if you don't want your life to be ravished by poverty. Nobody will employ a lazy man. The idol man is not needed but the workaholic is in high demand. Even if your company wants to promote a few of its workers, it is the workaholic they will look for. I could almost hear the CEO saying to the management board "I need a workaholic, do you know any?" If the board is to go on a search for two or three people among the junior staff to be promoted to senior staff, would you be workaholic enough to be selected? Until you become a workaholic, your chances of getting to the top remain slim. The workaholic will be preferred to you. Let me proof this to you using the life of a man called Tim cook.

TIM COOK, A WORKAHOLIC

Steve Jobs left incredibly big shoes for Tim Cook to fill. However, the man got the top job for a reason. He's always been a workaholic, Fortune reports that he begins sending emails at 4:30 in the morning.

A profile in Gawker reveals that he's the first in the office and last to leave. He used to hold staff meetings on Sunday night in order to prepare for Monday.

The most valuable tech company on Earth has a new boss, and it's Tim Cook, an intensely private and soft-spoken man who is taking over the role of CEO from one of the most iconic personalities on the planet. But who is Tim Cook? What's he like? What's he done to deserve the job? And can Apple really succeed without Steve Jobs at the helm?

To the latter question, the answer is a resounding yes. In fact, Tim Cook has arguably been running Apple's day-to-day operations for years. He has been more integral than anyone else in the company short of Steve himself in turning Apple around from a dying and moribund PC maker into the unstoppable juggernaut the company is today. Here's what you need to know.

- The son of a shipyard worker, Tim Cook was born on November 1, 1960 in Robertsdale, Alabama.

- Cook earned a Bachelor of Science degree in Industrial Engineering from Auburn University. He also has an MBA from Duke University as a Fuqua Scholar, which he achieved in 1988.

- Cook worked at IBM for 12 years starting in 1982.

- At IBM, Tim Cook was known for his dedication, working over Christmas and New Year holidays just so that IBM could complete its orders for the year.

- Within IBM, Cook was known for his geniality with his old IBM boss Richard Daugherty once saying of Cook that he had "a manner that really caused people to enjoy working with him."

- In 1994, Tim Cook joined Intelligent Electronics' computer reseller division, where he racked up his first position as COO.

- After selling the computer reseller division to Ingram Micro in 1997, Tim Cook went on to Compaq.

- Steve Jobs recognizes talent when he sees it, and after meeting Cook, poached him just six months into his career at Compaq.

- Tim Cook came to Apple in 1998. His first position was as the Senior Vice President of Worldwide Operations. In that position, Cook revolutionized Apple's supply chain and built strong relationships with external manufacturers.

- Tim Cook is a notorious workaholic. He reportedly starts emailing his colleagues at 4:30am every day and used to hold Sunday night telephone meetings with managers to prepare for the week ahead. Cook has been integral in making Apple the most profitable PC maker on Earth.

- In 2004, Tim Cook took over the Macintosh division at Apple and oversaw the migration of Macs from PowerPC to Intel chips.

- It was while being the head of the Mac division in 2004 that Tim Cook first took over for Steve Jobs and became interim CEO while Jobs went in for pancreatic surgery.

- In 2007, Tim Cook was promoted to COO.

- Two years later, in 2009, Tim Cook again took over as CEO when Steve Jobs took medical leave in order to get a liver transplant.

- Despite the fact that he was clearly being groomed for the job since at least 2004, Tim Cook never thought he'd be made CEO. He once famously said, "Come on, replace Steve? No. He's irreplaceable... That's something people have to get over. I see Steve there with grey hair in his 70s, long after I'm retired."

Today Tim cook is Apple's CEO. Why was Tim Cook the one that was chosen to succeed Steve Jobs? Do you think he deserves the job? The affirmative answer is found in the profile you just read. He is a workaholic and that alone qualified him for the job and position of CEO. It was because he was more diligent than everyone else. Steve Jobs must have been screaming in his heart "I need a workaholic, do you know any?" before he stumbled upon Tim cook, employed him and promoted him. That is the heart cry of every employer and manager "I need a workaholic do you know any". Even if they don't say it out, just know it is always in their heart. Nobody wants to hand over his company to a man who would destroy it out of laziness. Nobody gives his empire to the slothful man. Everybody wants to be succeeded by a workaholic. If you were the boss, would you hand over to a lazy person or to a diligent one? Of course to the diligent. That puts the lazy man in a disadvantaged position. No wonder his path is full of thorns and pain all the days of his life. Urgently become a workaholic else you will regret it.

REFUSE TO BECOME A WORKAHOLIC
AND YOU LOSE YOUR JOB

One thing that will certainly happen to you if you refuse to become a workaholic is that you will lose your job and will be moving from one job to another because nobody wants to retain a non-workaholic for ever. People will want to get rid of you as fast as they could once they notice that you are a lazy person. Everywhere you work, you will never have enough salary, and you will always be complaining and regretting that you are not being paid enough. No employer wants to increase the salary of an indolent employee. If you are not a workaholic, you will soon be retrenched from your office. You will be condemned to a life of perpetual pain. Your life is going to be littered with sorrows and regrets. Therefore there is no option than to become a Workaholic, which is the only way to live the kind of life that you dream of. If you don't work hard, you will suffer hard. If you keep running from hard work at your office or always sleeping on duty, I assure you, it won't be long before you will lose your job. You will be replaced by someone who is serious with life. A workaholic will take your place. If you are already jobless and you are not a workaholic, don't bother looking for a job because sooner than you think, you will be retrenched because of laziness. Go and cultivate diligence in your character first of all and jobs will come looking for you.

According to a report in 2012, Britain's army of administrators were to do a civil service reform by sacking all lazy and ineffective workers. This is how the story was captured by a reporter:

"Now even more lazy and ineffective civil servants face losing their jobs in sweeping reforms"

Tens of thousands more civil servants face losing their jobs over the next three years under sweeping reforms which will see the size of Whitehall slashed by a quarter, ministers were told yesterday.

Underperforming bureaucrats will be sacked or go un-replaced when they retire under plans to reduce the number of civil servants to around 380,000 by 2015"

Now look at that report above and tell me where the lazy man stands. He stands at a risk and at a lost. He will definitely lose his job.

> *Failure is not our only punishment for laziness;*
> *there is also the success of others.*
> JULES RENARD

If you refuse to become a workaholic you will lose your job and someone else who is diligent will replace you. In societies where only hard work is rewarded, the lazy man is as good as dead. He will live a life of poverty and regret. Such societies where hard work is valued develop faster than places like my country Nigeria where people celebrate laziness. Our civil service is littered with indolent and lethargic workers. They come to work late and leave early. They choose whatever day they like to come to work and don't show up on other working days. Many are ghost workers yet receive salaries at the end of the month. What a country! No wonder we are the way we are. No wonder we a suffering economic recession and regression. Other nations are working hard to develop themselves while Nigeria civil service is littered with people who are celebrating indolence. My suggestion is that all such laziness should be discouraged and stopped. All lazy workers should be retrenched and replaced with Workaholics. If we really want a faster growth and development for our country, we must learn to reward diligence and punish laziness. If you live a lazy lifestyle, you will pay for it by losing your job later.

> *People who are in the habit of enjoying the comfort of inaction often pay a high price in the end.*
> DR T.P. CHIA

If you settle for laziness today you will pay a high price for it later whether you like it or not. The reason for laziness in most societies is because people just want to become successful instantly without working hard first. The problem with my countrymen is that they don't want to work hard now, they just need instant gratification. Nobody wants to work like a slave now and live like a king tomorrow.

WORK LIKE A SLAVE TODAY. LIVE LIKE A KING TOMORROW

Anyone that ever became great had to pay the price. If you won't, then you will pay the price of regret, which is perpetual suffering for the rest of your life. Because you never studied, you never worked hard to add value to yourself, now you're poor and you can't live in a favourable condition. It is because you didn't pay the price for greatness. People who don't want to suffer don't want to be great. If you must become great in life you must first become a workaholic.

> *"Responsibility is the price of greatness."*
> WINSTON S. CHURCHILL

Any form of greatness has its own price. That is the price of responsibility and hard work. You must become responsible for your success in life by paying the price of diligence. For my elevation in life, I needed to pay a price. It didn't matter how hard it was. It is the price for greatness that I am enjoying today. In my university days, I increased my study time to 6 hours and challenged myself that no matter my schedule for the day, I will lock myself up in the library for 6 hours every day to study. That was exactly what I did. I did this throughout my 7 years of studies and I did not only become the best student after graduation but I made a record that after 25 years of completion, nobody has been able to break that record. This was possible because I pushed myself to the limit. I was able to beat the Russian students and all the students from 99 countries through hard work. What was the hard work? Well, I went to the library every day while other students would go home, to parties or to sport centres. I was the only one who was just sitting there using the dictionary and I read all the books and I would not rise until I spent six hours studying everything every single day for six years, I spent six hours every day in the library. I didn't get to this stage of my life by miracles. I worked hard like a slave and today I am reaping the reward. There was no miracle but diligence. That's the only way you can become the first. Listen to me, what are you waiting for before you become a workaholic? You cannot become the first person automatically, you will only become the first when you pay the price.

While most people are dreaming of success, winners wake up and work hard to achieve it.

ANONYMOUS

The other day, I was telling a couple who are my disciples, who said life was difficult that yes life has to be difficult at this stage. You have to make up your mind that maybe in the next 5 or so years of your life, you are going to work like a slave so that you will live the rest of your life as a king. The fact that you are a Workaholic doesn't mean you are a slave or deprived. Most millionaires are Workaholics and it is not because they need money but it is just that work has become their second nature. Work because of the creativity and excitement you get from it. Work like a slave today and you will live like a king tomorrow.

Congratulations to you dear friends, for reading thus far, I believe you learnt something about what happens to you when you become a workaholic. In this chapter, I stated that everyone is in need of workaholics while no one wants to associate with the slothful man. Tim Cook became Apple's CEO because he was a workaholic and the only one qualified to take over from Steve Jobs. I urge you to urgently become a workaholic because that's the only way to increase your worth, value and demand.

In the next chapter, I am going to reveal to you how you could become your own prophet and predict your future. I am sure you don't want to miss that. See you in the next chapter.

NUGGETS FROM
CHAPTER SIX

1. The path of a lazy or slothful person will be littered with sharp thorns as if they are walking bear footed on thorns or nails but the way of the up right is a high way

2. Everybody is looking for a Workaholic who will sit down and do all the work, who will not leave until all the jobs are done

3. Nobody wants a lazy man but everybody is ready to pay whatever it takes to get a workaholic.

4. A workaholic doesn't look for jobs, jobs look for him. Employers would retrench a lazy man just to get in a workaholic.

5. If you don't become a workaholic, nobody will need you. The whole world is looking for a workaholic.

6. Until you become a workaholic, your chances of getting to the top remain slim. The workaholic will be preferred to you.

7. Nobody gives his empire to the slothful. Everybody wants to be succeeded by a workaholic.

8. One thing that will certainly happen to you if you refuse to become a workaholic is that you will lose your job and will be moving

from one job to another because nobody
wants to retain a non-workaholic for ever.

9. People will want to get rid of you as fast as they
could once they notice that you are a lazy person.

10. There is no option than to become a
Workaholic, which is the only way to live
the kind of life that you dream of.

PRINCIPLES FROM
CHAPTER SIX

1. If you are already jobless and you are not a workaholic, don't bother looking for a job because sooner than you think, you will be retrenched because of laziness.

2. Go and cultivate hard work in your character first of all and jobs will come looking for you.

3. In societies where only hard work is rewarded, the slothful man is as good as dead. He will live a life of poverty and regret.

4. Societies where hard work is valued develop faster than places like my country Nigeria where people celebrate laziness.

5. If we really want a faster growth and development for our country, we must learn to reward Workaholics and punish slothfulness.

6. Anyone that ever became great had to pay the price. If you won't, then you will pay the price of regret, which is perpetual suffering for the rest of your life.

7. People who don't want to suffer don't want to be great. If you must become great in life you must first become a workaholic.

8. You cannot become the first person

automatically, you will only become
the first when you pay the price.

9. Most millionaires are Workaholics and it is
not because they need money but it is just
that work has become their second nature.

10. Work because of the creativity and excitement
you get from it. Work like a slave today
and you will live like a king tomorrow.

FOR THE WORKAHOLIC, LIFE IS PREDICTABLE

D ear friends, welcome to the seventh chapter of this book. It will amaze you to find in this chapter that you don't need a prophet in your life because you can become one. You can predict your own future and your predictions will be right. Read on friends, as I show you how to do it.

YOU DON'T NEED A PROPHET

With hard work, you can become your own prophet. You can predict the outcome of your life every month or every year. Workaholics do not run after prophets, they become their own prophets. In fact they are too busy working to have time for prophets. They know how much money their diligence will fetch them at the end of the month.

I am going to proof to you that for you not to be a Workaholic has consequences and you will be paying a high price for it and that for the workaholic, his future is sure and secured. He predicts his future and it gets his predictions right.

Proverbs 12:24a says that the hand of the diligent will rule.

The Bible already said it. If you are a workaholic you will rule in life. You don't need a prophet to tell you that. Just become diligent and your success can be predicted by you. Even at your work place, you could predict your promotion.

For example, if you have two workers; one is lazy and the other a Workaholic, who will you put in charge as the boss? Of course it will be the Workaholic. That is why for the Workaholic, life is predictable and the prediction is that, the person who works hard is going to be exalted or promoted whether you like it or not. Can you imagine a situation where by one of your workers tells you to reduce his work load or hours for the day or asks you to give his work to another worker because it is too much! How are you going to keep this kind of worker? And then you have another worker who says, I have finished my work before the deadline so give me another one to do. Which one of these workers will you promote? The Workaholic is the one going to be promoted and this is just the way life is. The diligent man will always be successful.

With hard work, life is predictable. You can tell who will become great tomorrow and who will not and your predictions will come true. Let me show you that life is predictable for the workaholic using the story below.

THE WILLIAM SISTERS: HOW THEY SUCCEEDED

Venus and Serena Williams were up hitting tennis balls at 6 A.M from the time they were 7 and 8 years old

The Williams sisters, who have dominated women's tennis for many years, were all but raised on the court.

From an extremely young age, their life was, as described to the New York Times "...Get up, 6 o'clock in the morning, and go to the tennis court, before school. After school, go to tennis..." The Williams family was built around propelling the two towards success in the sport.

EARLY LIFE

American tennis player Serena Jameka Williams was born on September 26, 1981, in Saginaw, Michigan. The youngest of Richard and Oracene Williams's five daughters, Serena Williams, along with her sister Venus, would grow up to become one of the sport's great champions.

Serena's father—a former sharecropper from Louisiana determined to see his two youngest girls succeed—used what he'd gleaned from tennis books and videos to instruct Serena and Venus on how to play the game. At the age of 3, practicing on a court not far from the family's new Compton, California, home, Serena withstood the rigors of daily two-hour practices from her father. Serena and Venus cut their teeth on the game of tennis and the requirements for persevering in a tough climate.

Friends, I am sure you can agree with me that for a 3 year old child to go through 2hrs of rigorous training every day is the height of diligence. There is no way that child will not grow up to become a genius in whatever area of life he or she has been trained in. The life of such a child could easily be predicted with accuracy. That is why the life of a workaholic is predictable. The same principle of diligence will work for anybody irrespective of his race or geographical location.

By 1991, Serena was 46-3 on the junior United States Tennis Association tour, and ranked first in the 10-and-under division. Sensing his girls needed better instruction to become successful professionals, he moved his family again—this time to Florida. There, Richard let go of some of his coaching responsibilities, but not the management of Serena's and Venus's career. Wary of his daughters burning out too quickly, he scaled back their junior tournament schedule.

TENNIS STAR

In 1995, Serena turned pro. Two years later, she was already No. 99 in the world rankings—up from No. 304 just 12 months before. A year later, she graduated from high school, and almost immediately inked a $12 million shoe deal with Puma. In 1999, she beat out her sister in their race to the family's first Grand Slam win, when she captured the U.S. Open title.

It set the stage for a run of high-powered, high-profile victories for both Williams sisters. With their signature style and play, Venus and Serena changed the look of their sport as well. Their sheer power and athletic ability overwhelmed opponents, and their sense of style and presence made them standout celebrities on the court.

In 2002, Serena won the French Open, the U.S. Open, and Wimbledon, defeating Venus in the finals of each tournament. She captured her first Australian Open in 2003, making her one of only six women in the Open era to complete a career Grand Slam. The win also fulfilled her desire to hold all four major titles simultaneously to comprise what she'd dubbed "The Serena Slam." In 2008, she won the U.S. Open and teamed with Venus to capture a second women's doubles Olympic gold medal at the Beijing Games.

Dear friends, having read the rigorous daily training lifestyle these sisters were exposed to from the age of 7 and 8, do you think they needed a prophet to predict their greatness in future? No they didn't. Hard-work predicted their life's success. Their father already knew they would be great because of the kind of hard work he had passed them through. People who run after prophets for predictions are lazy people and my country is full of them. Any child who wakes up 6am to learn whatever skills before going to school and continues when he returns from school every day will certainly become a genius in that skill. It doesn't matter what skill it is. The principle of diligence works wherever it is applied. It always produces positive results and its outcome can always be predicted. The Williams were being taught from books and videos of tennis from such an early age. There was no force on the face of the earth that could stop them from becoming great. For the workaholic, there is no limitation to his greatness. Heaven backs him up to succeed.

QUEEN OF THE COURT

By 2009, Williams had released a new autobiography, Queen of the Court, and won her place back atop the world's rankings, winning both the 2009 Australian Open singles (for the fourth time) and Wimbledon 2009 singles (for the third time). She also won the doubles matches at both the Australian Open and Wimbledon that year.

By early 2010, she won the Australian Open singles and doubles matches, as well as her fourth Wimbledon singles championship.

Williams stumbled badly at the 2012 French Open, enduring a first-round loss for the first time at a major tournament. But she was back in top form in London that summer, defeating 23-year-old Agnieszka Radwanska in an emotional three sets to claim her fifth Wimbledon singles title and first major championship in two years. Following the win, Williams rushed to her family in the stands, with tears in her eyes, and hugged them for several seconds. In a post-Wimbledon interview with ESPN, she was asked whether she thought she could top the win, and answered: "Are you kidding? The [2012] U.S. Open, the Australian Open, the French Open, Wimbledon 2013."

At the 2012 Summer Olympic Games, Serena beat Maria Sharapova to take her first gold medal in women's singles. The next day, she claimed her fourth overall Olympic gold medal by teaming with Sister Venus to defeat Czech Republic stars Andrea Hlavackova and Lucie Hradecka in women's doubles.

Williams continued her winning streak to her next Grand Slam event. In September 2012, she beat out rival Victoria Azarenka to take the singles title at the U.S. By this time, Williams had captured 15 Grand Slam singles titles and 13 Grand Slam doubles titles. "I would like to leave a mark," Williams once said about her standing in the tennis world. "I think obviously I will, due to the fact that I'm doing something different in tennis. But I don't think I could ever reach something like a Martina Navratilova — I don't think I'd ever play that long—but who knows? I think I'll leave a mark regardless."

At the U.S. Open, Williams made a strong showing. She knocked out her younger rival Sloane Stephens in the fourth round before upending Azarenka to clinch the U.S. Open title. It was the second year in a row that the pair had faced off in the finals.

Williams clinched her third straight and sixth overall U.S. Open singles title in 2014 by defeating her good friend Caroline Wozniacki. Her winning ways carried into the New Year, as she beat Sharapova to claim the 2015 Australian Open championship. At the French Open in June, Williams managed to overcome illness to win the tournament for the third time and claim her 20th Grand Slam singles title, good for third place all-time.

"When I was a little girl, in California, my father and my mother wanted me to play tennis," she told the crowd in French after her victory. "And now I'm here, with 20 Grand Slam titles."

Dear friends, do you think it was via miracles that the William sisters got to the height of their career? Do you think it was God's favour that made them win as much trophies and gold medals as they won? Well, if you are a Nigerian I guess your answer would be yes. The reason is because Nigerians think without God nothing can be done. Well, if it was God who did it for them, why did he decide to do it for only Serena Williams and her sister? Why didn't God do it for other players and why hasn't a Nigerian won any of such Wimbledon games? If God did it for only the William sisters, that means God doesn't like the other Tennis players like he likes Serena and her sister. In my opinion, God would have been found to show favouritism if that were true. But the truth is that, you and I know that God doesn't show favouritism. He is not a respecter of persons but a rewarder of principles. I therefore submit that the William Sisters got to that height in life because of a principle they obeyed from an early age. That is the principle of hard work. The principle of diligence. It is their hard work that God rewarded. It was diligence that predicted their future. I have written in this book before that any man who is diligent in his work shall stand before kings and not before ordinary men just as the bible stated. Therefore these sisters became the most popular and most celebrated Tennis players thanks to hard work. They became renown because they urgently became workaholics from childhood. There is no other way to explain their quick rise to the top of their career if not to agree that they were propelled by hard work.

On July 9, 2016, Williams defeated Kerber 7-5, 6-3 at Wimbledon and winning her 22nd grand slam title. Just hours after her singles win, Williams and her older sister Venus won the doubles championship at Wimbledon, their sixth Wimbledon win together.

With her 23rd win, she surpassed Steffi Graf's record and captured the world number one ranking.

Dear friends, champions are born out of hard work. Champions are only champions because they are Workaholics. Even before they become champions, you could predict that they would be, looking at how hard they work. If you desire to be a champion like Serena Williams you must pay the price of diligence. Whatever you do in life, put hard work into it and you will reap success. Don't just wish you were successful. Work hard to become successful.

> *"You don't need to wish harder, you need to work harder."*
>
> AMIT KALANTRI

If you have kids and you want them to become great and successful in life, turn them into Workaholics from an early age so that tomorrow you will not need to run from one church to another looking for prophets and miracles. Expose them to hard work now so that they will not become liabilities to society tomorrow. With hard work you can predict their future and it will be so.

A BETTER AND A BRIGHTER LIFE

Dear friends, you may be going through a tough and impoverished life and are asking yourself "when will life get better?" Well, life will not get better by itself unless you make it better. The future doesn't become brighter by itself. It takes hard work to make the future brighter. Anybody you see, who is living a better life than you, must have at one point in life paid a price for it and that is the price of hard work. Nobody was born with a better life than you. Nobody was born to be greater or better than you. Those who are greater or better than you have only become better because they worked harder than you. They paid a greater price than you. A better life can only be bought through diligence. Greatness is an attainment that is bought with the currency of hard work. The secret to a better and brighter life is to work harder than anyone else and become a workaholic. Stop complaining about your life if you are not ready to become a workaholic. Work hard. Add value to yourself. Make yourself the best in what you do. Make yourself competitive and you will be surprised how quickly your life will become better and brighter. Life will only become brighter for the diligent and not for the empty dreamer. The empty dreamers die in their dreams and never see their dreams come to pass. Diligence is the only thing that makes big dreams come true. In Proverbs 21:25, the bible continues to say that, the lazy man dies in his expectations for his hands refuse to labour. So, be a Workaholic or be ridiculed in life. You will also live a life of depression and murmuring if you refuse to become a workaholic. In Proverbs 13:4 the bible says that the soul of a lazy man desires and has nothing but the soul of the diligent shall be made rich. So instead of you just living in your dreams, thinking that one day God will bless you or favour you, just get up and begin to work hard and diligently. If you do that, your diligence will make a way for you. Your life will only get brighter and better if you become a workaholic and a diligent person.

> *"To become a better you, be diligent and never let the charms of procrastination and excuses seduce you to fall for mediocrity."*
> ISRAELMORE AYIVOR

As I bring this chapter to a close, I would like to remind you that you don't need a Prophet, you don't need a miracle because you can become your own prophet and make your miracles. The man who is a workaholic is superior to the man who is waiting for miracles and depending on prophets for his success in life. Urgently become a workaholic and your life will become better and brighter.

In the next chapter, I am going to reveal to you that despite the call to become workaholics, it is better to become a workaholic in your area of calling. Follow me to the next chapter as I show you how to work the greatest kind of work.

NUGGETS FROM
CHAPTER SEVEN

1. With hard work, you can become your own prophet. You can predict the outcome of your life every month or every year.

2. Workaholics do not run after prophets, they become their own prophets.

3. If you are a workaholic you will rule in life. You don't need a prophet to tell you that.

4. For the Workaholic, life is predictable and the prediction is that, the person who works hard is going to be exalted or promoted.

5. The diligent man will always be successful.

6. With hard work, life is predictable.

7. The principle of diligence will work for anybody irrespective of his race or geographical location.

8. People who run after prophets for predictions are lazy people.

9. The principle of diligence works wherever it is applied. It always produces positive results and its outcome can always be predicted.

10. For the workaholic, there is no limitation to his greatness. Heaven backs him up to succeed.

PRINCIPLES FROM
CHAPTER SEVEN

1. Champions are born out of hard work.

2. Champions are only champions because they are Workaholics.

3. Whatever you do in life, put hard work into it and you will reap success.

4. Life will not get better by itself unless you make it better.

5. The future doesn't become brighter by itself. It takes hard work to make the future brighter.

6. Those who are greater or better than you have only become better because they worked harder than you. They paid a greater price than you.

7. A better life can only be bought through diligence. Greatness is an attainment that is bought with the currency of hard work.

8. The secret to a better and brighter life is to work harder than anyone else and become a workaholic.

9. Work hard. Add value to yourself. Make yourself the best in what you do. Make yourself competitive and you will be surprised how quickly your life will become better and brighter.

10. Your life will only get brighter and better if you become a workaholic and a diligent person.

THE GREATEST KIND OF WORK

Dear friends, having read from chapter one up till this point in this book, I believe it is obvious to you now that you must become a workaholic. However it is better to become a workaholic in your area of calling and I am going to show you how you can become as great as Michelangelo and Beethoven who worked the greatest kind of work.

WORKING ON YOUR CALLING AND PURPOSE.

Unfortunately when people are talking about work, they talk about job but I am talking about the kind of work that will add value to you, the one that is your calling or destiny to make you fulfilled and carry out your goals in life. I mean the one God created you for. You were not created for a job you were created for work and the kind of work I am talking about is the one connected to your life's purpose and calling. Hence my call for you to urgently become a workaholic is not for some job but for the fulfilment of your purpose. To be a workaholic for your boss at job has only a little benefit compared to being a workaholic on your area of calling and for yourself. When you become a workaholic in your area of calling, you soon realize that you have become so good that you are now qualified to be a boss and an employer of labour. People who work hard at their job will be promoted but will still remain as employees under a boss. But when you are a workaholic in your area of calling, you are the employer not the employee. You determine what you do with your life and how much you get at the end of the month. Your salary is not determined by someone else or the government. In addition to that, you feel fulfilled and accomplished when you do the greatest kind of hard work, which is working hard for your purpose instead of for a job description. Most people who work hard at their jobs are not truly satisfied or fulfilled neither do they love what they do. They only work hard so as to get salary at the end of the month. To not be a Workaholic is very disruptive which means you will be living a life of deception thinking that you are out smarting others and will still get paid for it.

History is full of people who were diligent in their area of calling and purpose and who thanks to hard work became great and renowned. Every one of us should be so diligent in whatever we've been called to do such that even after we exit the earth, generations to come will still benefit from the legacy we left behind.

> "If a man is called to be a street sweeper, he should sweep streets even as a Michelangelo painted, or Beethoven composed music or Shakespeare wrote poetry. He should sweep streets so well that all the hosts of heaven and earth will pause to say, 'Here lived a great street sweeper who did his job well."
>
> MARTIN LUTHER KING JR.

Why do you think Martin Luther King Jr. mentioned these great names? Why is he asking everyone to do what they have been called to do and do it with all diligence like Michelangelo, Beethoven and Williams Shakespeare did? It is my belief that these men would have been so diligent that no one else could be compared to them when the idea of hard work is discussed. To proof that to you, I want us to look at a brief story of Michelangelo and Beethoven.

THE WORKAHOLIC MICHELANGELO: CALLED TO PAINT

Michelangelo Buonarroti was born on March 6, 1475, in Caprese, Italy. His father used to beat him because he didn't do his lessons but drew all the time.

He didn't want the boy to become an artist. He considered an artist's trade to be beneath the family dignity. But finally, since Michelangelo was so stubborn, he apprenticed him (1488) to a painter (Ghirlandaio), who afterward claimed to have taught him all he knew.

Michelangelo was exceptionally good at drawing and copying things. He impressed everyone with his version of an engraving by a German artist (Schongauer).

Michelangelo learned about sculpture (1489) at a school set up in the palace of a rich and powerful duke named Lorenzo de Medici. After only a few days he surprised Lorenzo with a perfect stone copy of a faun. Lorenzo invited him to live in his palace, gave him a place at his table, and a violet robe to wear. He lived there for three years and, while carving his first works in marble, sat in classes with Lorenzo's sons, taught by the great teachers (Humanists) of Florence.

Lorenzo de Medici suddenly became sick and died (1492).Lorenzo's successor, his son Piero, kept Michelangelo at the palace and ordered him to make a snowman. Michelangelo made his first trip to the quarries of Carrara to get the marble for his next great statue, the Pietà.

Florence became a republic (they executed Savonarola) and Michelangelo went back home. He sculpted a marble Cupid (1495) and treated it to look old. A crooked merchant sold it as an antique to a Cardinal in Rome. When he found out, the Cardinal returned the Cupid to the agent. He did not blame Michelangelo but he didn't keep this statue either. He invited Michelangelo to live at his palace in Rome and commissioned a life-sized statue of Bacchus, the God of wine.

Michelangelo returned to Florence to try to get a big marble block that was being handed out by the city governor. It had been standing around in a yard for years and had a hole through it, so it was considered worthless. He took measurements and designed for it a statue of David, the shepherd boy who killed Goliath with a stone from his sling. David is seventeen feet high. Michelangelo carved it in just eighteen months and it was set up in front of the Town Hall (Palazzo Della Signoria) of Florence.

Julius II, as soon as he was elected Pope (1505), wanted to do great things and called Michelangelo to Rome to design and build his tomb. Michelangelo came up with a complex design with forty statues, which delighted the Pope. In great spirits, Michelangelo went to Carrara to quarry the marble. He returned after eight months and set up a shop near the Vatican. The Pope used to drop by his workshop to chat and see how things were coming along. Suddenly the Pope changed his mind about the tomb and canceled the project. Michelangelo was so shocked and angered that he destroyed his models, left Rome by night, and went back home to Florence (1506).

THE CEILING OF THE SISTINE CHAPEL

Then Julius called Michelangelo to Rome to paint the ceiling of the Sistine Chapel (1508). "But I'm not a painter," Michelangelo protested. He had painted very little and the Pope was asking him to fill three thousand square feet of ceiling. Julius wouldn't take no for an answer. Painting the ceiling of the Sistine Chapel took four years and was the hardest thing Michelangelo ever did. He worked alone, pushing himself to the limit every day. He ate old bread and slept in his work clothes. "I have no time for friends," he wrote his father.

Dear friends, that is hard work right there. To push yourself to the limit. Every day he had to mix up a batch of plaster and trowel it on the wall, and had to hurry to finish his painting else the plaster would dry up. It takes a lot of hard work to paint a ceiling because everything has to be lifted, scribed, and painted above your head.

He stood on the wooden plank of the scaffolding sixty feet in the air and worked looking up. You could imagine how much weight would be on his neck looking up for four years working on just one project. Michelangelo was no doubt a workaholic.

When the ceiling was only half-finished, the impatient Pope ordered Michelangelo to take down the scaffolding and open the chapel to the public. The paintings created a great stir in Rome and all Italy. They illustrated the saga of Man from his creation to the coming of Christ.

The public crowded into the chapel and spread the news that the paintings were the greatest thing they had ever seen. The figures showed a new kind of beauty and power. Each of them was a masterpiece in its conception and colours. Michelangelo's vision was overwhelming.

Pope Clement ordered him to paint the altar wall of the Sistine Chapel. It took him eight years to finish The Last Judgment (1541) because of interruptions for other work and illness. He fell off the scaffold once and was in bed for months. It was his last great painting. But when he was over seventy he did two more huge frescoes in the Vatican: the Conversion of St. Paul and the Crucifixion of St. Peter.

At last, he finished the Julius Tomb. In fact, most of it was sculpted by his helpers. But the central figure—the Moses— is one of Michelangelo's most powerful statues.

The last important job he had, which occupied him for years when he was old, was St. Peter's Basilica. Two Popes made him the official architect. An assistant helped him build a model for the dome.

He died at 89 (1564) after a few days with a fever. His nephew took his body back home to Florence. The funeral was one of the biggest Florence ever saw. More than a hundred artists attended.

THE FIRST DUTY OF A WORKAHOLIC

The first thing you want to do to as a workaholic is to discover your area of calling. That should be the first duty of every workaholic. The secret of all greatness is to discover what you were born to do in life and then do it with all your strength. You must find out your gifts and talents and work hard to perfect them. For Michelangelo, he discovered that his own gift was in drawing artworks. He was able to find out why he was born and worked relentlessly hard to fulfil it. When you want to become great, you have to become a workaholic in your area of purpose and calling instead of just living your life for a job description. What I mean is that working hard to improve and fulfil your purpose is the greatest type of hard work. It is a quicker and more fulfilling road to success than just working for a job description from your boss or your government. All the great names in history were hardworking and became workaholics but not for a job description. Michelangelo knew he was called to paint and became a workaholic in his area of calling. Beethoven knew he was called to compose music and dedicated his hard work to doing that. The same could be said of Shakespeare who wrote poetry. So, the way to work the greatest kind of work is to first discover your gifts, talents, and calling and that will help you to know where you should channel your hard work. It is your gifting and talents that dictate to you where you should invest your energy and hard work. It was his talent that gave him direction as to what to do with his life. Therefore you must find out what you were born to do and become a workaholic fulfilling it. Self - discovery is the key to knowing where to channel your energy. The starting point for greatness is to work hard on your calling and purpose in life.

From the story above, we could notice a few things about Michelangelo that made him great. The first thing we could notice about him was that he had a passion and love for drawings. He was obsessed with drawing. In fact he was addicted to art work. He would rather draw pictures than solve his assignments at school. That was a pointer to what he was born to do. The second thing which was the most striking thing about him was that he drew all the time. In order words, he was a workaholic artist. He converted most of his time into drawing and perfecting his skills and talent in the world of art. Michelangelo was exceptionally good at drawing because he worked so hard to learn and perfect the act of drawing until he became a workaholic. There is no great person in history who gained mastery in a particular skill without first investing hard work into perfecting that skill.

Because he worked hard to add value to himself, he became so good that he was invited to the palace of Lorenzo. Only a man who is exceptionally skillful can stand before kings. Only men who through hard work have become the best in what they do are fit to sit and dine with kings. Whatever it is you have been called to do, if you will become a workaholic in perfecting it, you will soon be reckoned among the great in your society.

Dear friends, there was no way Michelangelo could achieve such greatness if he was not diligent. His works were masterpieces and everyone who saw them were mesmerized by them. People were astounded by his artistic paintings because he was diligent in gaining the mastery over his talents. He became a master of his skills only because he worked so hard to develop them. It was thanks to diligence that Michelangelo became great. You could see that he was very hardworking in his days as attested to by one of his quotes below.

> *"If people knew how hard I had to work to gain my mastery, it would not seem so wonderful at all."*
>
> MICHELANGELO BUONARROTI

In fact, Michelangelo could be in the Sistine Chapel for many months just working on a project. That is hard work right there.

Some projects took him eight years to finish, others took four years. It was diligence that gave him the persistence to work for so long on his projects. So, dear friends, if you really desire greatness, you should make up your mind to be a hard worker. You should learn to use your time to better your skills and talents through the instrumentality of work like Michelangelo did. You can gain the mastery over any skill if only you will make up your mind to work hard on it. If you want to be great, you must learn the secret of great men. They all understood that it is through working hard to fulfil one's purpose that greatness can be attained. Hence they all became workaholics in their area of purpose and calling.

The Workaholic Beethoven: Called
To Compose Music

Ludwig Van Beethoven lived for only 56 years. He became a workaholic in his own land of promise and that is why he became one of the best musical composers of all time.

Beethoven was born on 16th, December 1770 in Bonn of Germany. His father was a singer in a local palace choir.

Beethoven couldn't afford to go to school because of his poor family background. However, he had an extravagant love for music at a very tender age. He was potentially gifted in music. As a result, Beethoven had to practice playing clavicorn and violin day and night under his father's pressure.

He was able to invest about fifty thousand hours into his musical calling and became one of the best musical composers in history. That is what I consider real hard work, to invest as much time rehearsing endlessly.

It was this constant practice every day and night that made him exceptionally skillful. He constantly worked hard on himself, learning and perfecting new skills. He didn't live an indolent life like other children but he disciplined himself under his father to learn and become the best in his area of gifting. He would overwork himself beyond his father's demands and often refuse to stop playing the piano when his father wanted to finish rehearsals for the day. He was so passionately in love with the chords he played that he wouldn't want the practice sessions to end. He was a workaholic even at an early age.

Even though he was from a poor background, he didn't allow that deter him from becoming a workaholic. Poverty is irrelevant when there is hard work. It is hard work that determines greatness not family background. You don't have to be born into a rich family to become great in life. You only need to become a workaholic. Therefore no one can use poverty as an excuse for not becoming great. Beethoven despite his poor background became great by working hard and adding value to himself. He worked so hard to gain the mastery over his musical skills. He was diligent in refining and perfecting his skills.

Beethoven had a performance on a stage for the first time when he was only seven years old and he made a huge success. Some famous musicians considered him as the second Mozart. Beethoven learned how to compose music from Nifo and published his first work named Concerto in A minor when he was 11. He went to Vienna to learn how to compose music from Mozart and Haydn.

Instead of just going to a normal school, he was wise enough to focus on his talents. Even though they were from a poor background, he was able to work hard to learn the act of composing music. He invested his life into his purpose and became one of the best in the world. He became great thanks to the power of hard work. He regularly added value to himself and that is why he was able to give birth to great music. You must understand that all great things come through hard work

Beethoven received his first success in 1800. Nevertheless, he was troubled with a terrible matter for years at that time. He found that he has become a deaf person. There couldn't be anything more terrible than that for a musician.

Despite his hearing loss, he was still able to compose many more beautiful music including The Second Symphonies from 1803 onward. His music was exceptionally unique and warm to the heart.

In 1823, he finished his masterpiece named The Ninth Symphonies. By the time his ninth symphonies was performed that night in Vienna, he was profoundly deaf. Many years later his music is still as powerful, overwhelming and brilliant as ever. The most intriguing thing about his music is the fact that the composer of such beautiful music was unable to hear. He did not use the fact that he lost his hearing as an excuse to waste his life, rather he kept on working hard and that hard work earned him greatness.

His music impacted the world and transformed many lives. It changed the history of music. He is regarded as one of the giants of classical music and his influence on subsequent generations of composers was profound but this is only because he became a workaholic who worked endlessly to add value to himself and to his generation.

"It seemed unthinkable for me to leave the world forever before I had produced all that I felt called upon to produce"

LUDWIG VAN BEETHOVEN

From his quote above you could see that he was intentional about all the music he produced. He wasn't just producing music, he understood that hard work was needed to be able to produce as much music as he was called to produce. He knew that which many people on earth do not know; that is the fact that life is only worth living if it is used to produce products for the good of humanity. Besides just working hard, Beethoven also understood that every man has been called to fulfil a specific assignment on earth within the time allocated to him to live on earth and that failure to do that will mean a wasted life. He understood his calling and soaked himself in it. He knew that the only way to live a life of no regret in this race of life is to work hard particularly in your area of calling.

> *"I know you have heard it a thousand times before, but it's true; hard work pays off. If you want to be good, you have to practice, practice, and practice. If you don't love something, then don't do it"*
> RAY BRADBURY

Do you intend to leave a legacy for future generations? If your answer is yes then you may want to start following the example of Beethoven. You may want to start focusing on investing your hard work into exploring your area of calling. It doesn't matter what your area of calling is, if you could work hard in it then you will be sure to become successful in it. The world awaits your success. Humanity lives in eager expectation of your greatness. Begin to work hard. Begin to gain the mastery over your talents and gifting. Become a workaholic. Do not leave the world without fulfilling your purpose. You can become great but only thanks to how much work you are able to do in your area of calling.

> *"Everybody wants to be famous, but nobody wants to do the work. I live by that. You grind hard so you can play hard. At the end of the day, you put all the work in, and eventually it will pay off. It could be in a year, it could be in 30 years, your hard work will pay off"*
> KEVIN HART

The quality of work you dedicate to your purpose is what determines your greatness. It is good to work for salary but it is better to work for your purpose. You cannot become great by working for a salary. To work for salary is to mortgage your life. It is to give out your life for a little compensation. You were not created to live your life for compensation. You were created to invest your life into your promise land, your area of calling. You, therefore, should be working only for your purpose and area of calling. The difference between working for a salary and working for your purpose is that when you work for a salary, you are exchanging your life just for some porridge, some little compensation in the form of salary. You are giving out your life but you are getting back only compensation that is called salary. Salary is the compensation you get for giving out your life. But when you choose your own land of promise, when you choose your own area of greatness, nobody determines what you earn per month or per year. When you choose your own area of calling and purpose, and you are working and converting your life into that your area of calling, you are not being compensated with salary. You become the boss over your own life. You are planting yourself and cultivating your own ground. You are investing your life into that your own land of promise.

The best way to becoming a workaholic is to find out your calling, find out your divine gifting and work hard on developing your gift and your calling. What I am saying is, be intentional! Be purposeful! Become a workaholic in your area of calling. Maybe God wants you to resolve the medical issues in your country or to discover something new in the computer industry or in the area of the economy, in the area of science or in politics. Just make sure you know your own calling and invest your hard work into fulfilling it.

When Michelangelo goes into his studio and starts to work on his project, he remains in solitude in that studio for two months, for three months, for six months. Just painting. What was he doing? He didn't want to lose any time. He didn't want to give room for any distractions. He was taking advantage of the gift of work. He was practicing the principle of hard work. That is why he is one of the greatest artists in history. He however invested his hard work only in his area of calling. He was investing his own life back into his own destiny. You must understand that your calling is your destiny.

He was not giving out his life to somebody to be compensated for. He was giving back his life into himself, into his own destiny and purpose. Therefore the quality of work he was able to invest into his life determined his greatness.

Michelangelo became great because of how much work he was able to invest into his promise land. For example, he will lock up himself in his studio for as much as six months. Why did he lock up himself there for such a long time? He didn't just want to work for eight hours per day like everyone else. He wasn't playing or joking with his destiny but was making sure that he worked harder and longer than everyone else in his area of calling. If you really want to be successful in life, you must invest quality amount of work into your purpose and land of calling. The more great work you invest into your purpose and calling, the more professional you become. So your success in life is directly proportional to how much work you are ready to invest into fulfilling your purpose.

As I round off this chapter, I want to remind you of all we've said in this chapter by charging you to invest maximum amount of hard work into refining your gift and become best at what you were called to do and you will be surprised how easily and quickly you will rise to the top. If you will invest the maximum amount of hard work into polishing and building your own land of promise, you will become great in life. You will become exceptional. You will become a specialist and the world would want to reckon with you.

You can never truly become successful in life if you do not discover your purpose in life and work hard to fulfil it. Therefore strive to discover why you exist and then begin to invest your energy and hard work into achieving it. Urgently become a workaholic in your calling. Find out your talents and gifts and invest your whole energy and hard work into perfecting them and success will become your second nature.

In the next chapter, I am going to be showing you the consequences of not becoming a workaholic.

NUGGETS FROM
CHAPTER EIGHT

1. You were not created for a job, you were created for work and the kind of work I am talking about is the one connected to your life's purpose and calling.

2. My call for you to urgently become a workaholic is not for some job but for the fulfilment of your purpose.

3. To be a workaholic for your boss at job has only a little benefit compared to being a workaholic on your area of calling and for yourself.

4. When you become a workaholic in your area of calling, you soon realize that you have become so good that you are now qualified to be a boss and an employer of labour.

5. When you are a workaholic in your area of calling, you are the employer not the employee.

6. You feel fulfilled and accomplished when you are diligent in your area of calling.

7. Every one of us should be so diligent in whatever we've been called to do such that even after we exit the earth, generations to come will still benefit from the legacy we left behind.

8. The first thing you want to do to work as a

workaholic is to discover your area of calling.

9. The secret of all greatness is to discover what you were born to do in life and then do it with all your strength.

10. You must find out your gifts and talents and work hard to perfect them.

PRINCIPLES FROM
CHAPTER EIGHT

1. When you want to become great, you have to become a workaholic in your area of purpose and calling instead of just living your life for a job description.

2. Working hard to improve and fulfil your purpose is the greatest type of hard work.

3. The way to work the greatest kind of work is to first discover your gifts, talents, and calling and that will help you to know where you should channel your hard work.

4. It is your gifting and talents that dictate to you where you should invest your energy and hard work.

5. You must find out what you were born to do and become a workaholic fulfilling it. Self-discovery is the key to knowing where to channel your energy

6. The starting point for greatness is to work hard on your calling and purpose in life.

7. There is no great person in history who gained mastery in a particular skill without first investing hard work into Perfecting that skill.

8. Only men who through hard work have become the best in what they do

are fit to sit and dine with kings.

9. Whatever it is you have been called to do, if you will become a workaholic in perfecting it, you will soon be reckoned among the great in your society.

10. If you want to be great, you must learn the secret of great men. They all understood that it is through working hard to fulfil one's purpose that greatness can be attained.

CONSEQUENCES OF NOT BEING A WORKAHOLIC

Having stressed the importance of hard work all through this book, I will now highlight the consequences of refusing to work hard and becoming a workaholic.

STOP WORKING AND EVERYTHING GOES WRONG

Friends, never get to a point in your life when you begin to think that you don't have to work. You will be signing up for a life full of crisis and challenges if you decide to stop working. In fact if you ever get to a point in life where you conclude that you don't need to work, things will go wild and wrong for you. Things go wrong for anybody that doesn't live a Workaholic lifestyle. The day you become reluctant to work, that is the day you die. Work is one of the greatest blessings given to us by God to be able to sustain life here on earth. The scriptures tells us to urgently become Workaholic or things will begin to go wrong in our lives.

In Proverbs 15:19, it says that, the way of the slothful is laid with thorns. In other words, a lazy person has troubles throughout his life. A slothful person is the one who works when he feels like it. He can be equated to a lazy person but a lazy person is worse than a slothful person. A slothful person works just enough to survive or make a living. So if you are not a Workaholic then you are a slothful person. Therefore from the bible verse above, the path of a slothful person is laid up with thorns. It is like walking on a straight road filled with thorns or nails. Can you imagine your path in life filled with arranged thorns and nails all the days of your life with you walking bear footed? That will be a terrible experience that no man would want to go through, but that is how your life will be if you refuse to become a workaholic. This is how the life of anybody who is not a workaholic will be, a life of constant pain and regrets. He will live a despicable life, a life of perpetual pain. If your life becomes like that, it means you don't have life at all. Look around you and in your own life, you will see that people who are not working 14-18 hours a day are always in one pain or the other. They are always depending on others because they don't have money. Anybody that does not work hard is always in pain of not having enough to provide the basic things in life. His life is full of struggles, regrets and pain. He will always be crying and bleeding from one bad thing or the other. Everything goes wrong for anyone who stops working or refuses to become a workaholic.

If you refuse to be a workaholic now, your mate or someone even younger than you will become your boss tomorrow and command you as he wants. You will be subjugated by those who have become workaholics. Workaholics will always rule over lazy people.

IS IT BAD TO BE A WORKAHOLIC?

The reason most people do not want to become workaholics is because, sometimes we think that to be a Workaholic is negative. Well, there might be some negative aspect of it but if you are not a Workaholic in this world, you will suffer more negative effects and repercussions. At least before you attain your breakthrough, you must be a Workaholic for a certain period of your life. Maybe a period of one, two or more years but you must become a workaholic to achieve anything great in life. You will need to be a Workaholic now so that you can relax a little bit later but only after you have attained your dream. But if you have never once been a workaholic, I urge you to urgently become a Workaholic now. If you don't, I am afraid you will regret it all your life.

Is it a bad thing to become a Workaholic? Well, I will leave you to answer that question by the time you finish reading this book. Even if people say that it is bad to be a workaholic, I can tell you for sure that it gives you more good things than bad. The result it offers you is more positive than negative and if you are not a Workaholic, the results are not very good. If you really want to know if it's bad to be a workaholic, ask Thomas Edison how he became one of the greatest geniuses that ever lived through hard work. If you think it's bad to be a workaholic, ask all the great men in history who became successful thanks to hard work.

COULD JESUS BE A WORKAHOLIC

You know Jesus equated work to teaching. All through his years of ministry, he was moving from place to place teaching people. He said once "I must work the works of him that sent me, while it is day: the night cometh, when no man can work" He understood the need for work and he worked all through his years of ministry. If being a work-aholic was bad, Jesus would not have become one himself

To some extent, Jesus could have been regarded as a Workaholic. If Jesus was a Workaholic, what then is your own excuse? He had all the anointing, blessings and direct access to God himself but he still worked. He never dreamt of not working unlike some of us who do not have direct access to God. There are so many people who are dreaming of not working. In fact most people in Africa especially in Nigeria are dreaming of not working but dream of becom-ing wealthy and influential in the future.

If you don't become a workaholic, you will regret the consequences. What then are the consequences of not being a workaholic? Well I will be glad to share some of them with you.

THE CONSEQUENCES OF NOT BEING A WORKAHOLIC ARE:

1. You Will Be Put To Forced Labour

Proverbs 12:24 says that the slothful man will be put to forced labour. This means that anybody who doesn't want to work will be controlled by others sitting on their neck, forcing them to work. So if you are not a Workaholic, you will be a slave. People will not pay you your salary if they don't make sure that you are working. You will be work-ing not out of joy or for satisfaction but out of compulsion because you are being paid a salary. You are going to be subdued to do the kind of work you don't want to do. If you refuse to become a workaholic, People will be ruling your life and you will be a servant which is disgrace.

2. If you are not a Workaholic, whether you like it or not, you are a dependant person.

You will always be dreaming and praying that someone will come and help you. You will always be hoping for a miracle. This is what the church is asking us to do, to be hoping and asking for miracles and wait for some help to come from somewhere. This is a symbol of laziness and it means that you have the culture of slothfulness. Hard working people take their destiny into their own hands and do not wait for some miracles. The results of your life depend on the amount of work you do and you have to tell yourself the truth that "if I don't work, I don't deserve to have it". If you are not working for it, you shouldn't live in deception that miracle will come from somebody or somewhere. These things can happen but even if it does, you will still be a slave to that person. Therefore a lazy person will be put under control.

3. Anybody that is not Workaholic is going to have a people-relationship problems.

There is going to be struggles in your relationship because you will be living in lack. This means that you will always need something from somebody. You will always be thinking that somebody needs to help you and that somebody will also be thinking: why is this person not working and always asking for something. This will happen even if you are families. They will say, I also have my problems and you will be angry asking them why they promised and didn't keep their promise. So anybody who is not a Workaholic is a conflict person.

4. Non-workaholics are like vinegar to the teeth and smoke to eyes

According to Proverbs 10:26, a Non-workaholic is like vinegar to the teeth and smoke to the eyes of those who sent him. A Lazy person will always have problems and challenges with leadership. This is because a non-workaholic is always under pressure. Their leaders are always dissatisfied and demand more from them which will get them annoyed. Non-workaholics always get annoyed at people who are demanding much from them and their bosses also get annoyed and frustrated at them and begin to demand more from them than what they can give.

5. They are not very responsible and they put their responsibility on other people.

Lazy people are irresponsible people and as a result of that, nothing gets done or done well. This kind of people are always in a bad relationship with people and are always unhappy thinking that nobody wants to help them or everybody is against them.

6. He always has excuses and complains.

He is always just nagging that everybody or things are bad. A hard worker takes responsibility and goes to work. Non-workaholics always and constantly give excuses as to why things are not done and people don't like such kind of persons

7. The Poverty of the Slothful

A slothful person is always poor. Because the bible says that the hands of a diligent person makes him rich but the hands of a lazy man brings poverty. So if you are not a Workaholic, you are most likely to stand a good chance of becoming poor. People will unfortunately look down on you. You will not be respected because others think that you are a parasite. So for you to change that attitude towards you, you need to change that character and urgently become a workaholic.

8. He always misses opportunity.

The indolent man is afraid of anything that looks like work. When opportunity comes he misses because he thinks that it is work. The Workaholic however easily recognises opportunity because he is always ready to work.

> "We often miss opportunity because it's dressed in overalls and looks like work"
> THOMAS A. EDISON

THE SLOTHFUL MAN IS A TIME WASTER

Slothful People are Time Wasters. A person who is not a workaholic will have time for frivolous things. He will be killing time instead of investing time. You can either spend, waste or invest time. People who invest time are the ones who are wise. Those who spend time are Mediocre and those who waste time are the fools. Unfortunately most people spend and waste time but we are supposed to be time investors. People who are slothful have time for empty stuffs.

They want to go to the movies, cinemas and the likes. They are always engaged in trivial things instead of converting that time into money to add value to themselves and others. They just want to enjoy life. Proverbs 21:25 says that the desire of the lazy person will kill him. Why? Because he is always just desiring to have this or that and when it doesn't come, he gets heart attack. A lazy person desires a thing but does nothing towards getting it and because of that, he lives a life of expectations. The lazy man's life is full of troubles and poverty because he does not know the value of time.

Time is the only commodity in life that cannot be bought, sold, borrowed, given out as a gift and it cannot be inherited. "Time is the scarcest resource and unless it is managed nothing else can be managed." -Peter F. Drucker

Having seen the consequences of not being a workaholic, I am sure you don't want to go through all of the sufferings and hardship that non workaholics go through. That means you will have to resolve to become a workaholic. In the next chapter, I am going to show you why you should urgently become a workaholic.

NUGGETS FROM
CHAPTER NINE

1. You will be signing up for a life full of crisis
    and challenges if you decide to stop working.

2. Things go wrong for anybody that
    doesn't live a Workaholic lifestyle.

3. The day you become reluctant to
    work, that is the day you die.

4. Work is one of the greatest blessings given to us
    by God to be able to sustain life here on earth.

5. This is how the life of anybody who
    is not a workaholic will be, a life of
    constant pain and regrets.

6. Anybody that does not work hard is
    always in pain of not having enough
    to provide the basic things in life.

7. If you refuse to be a workaholic now, your mate or
    someone even younger than you will become your
    boss tomorrow and command you as he wants.

8. Workaholics will always rule over lazy people.

9. If you don't become a workaholic, you
    will regret the consequences.

10. If you are not a Workaholic, you will be a slave.

PRINCIPLES FROM
CHAPTER NINE

1. If you refuse to become a workaholic, People will be ruling your life and you will be a servant which is disgrace.

2. Hard working people take their destiny into their own hands and do not wait for some miracles.

3. If you are not working for it, you shouldn't live in deception that miracle will come from somebody or somewhere

4. Lazy people are irresponsible people and as a result of that, nothing gets done or done well

5. A hard worker takes responsibility and goes to work. Non-workaholics always and constantly give excuses as to why things are not done.

6. So if you are not a Workaholic, you are most likely to stand a good chance of becoming poor.

7. The indolent man is afraid of anything that looks like work. When opportunity comes he misses because he thinks that it is work.

8. The Workaholic easily recognises opportunities because he is always ready to work.

9. Slothful People are Time Wasters. A person who is not a workaholic will

have time for frivolous things.

10. A lazy person desires a thing but does nothing towards getting it and because of that, he lives a life of expectations.

CHAPTER 10

URGENTLY BECOME
A WORKAHOLIC

Dear friends, I am delighted you've read through this book till the last chapter. I believe you must have learnt some principles of diligence and hard work that will propel you to greatness in life. I would love to remind you that a workaholic is anyone who has become addicted to work that he or she cannot live without working. Only men who love hard work are entitled to success in life. Success and greatness in life are gotten, only thanks to hard work. I do hope you still remember that Work is related to life and that without work there will be no life. I have stated in the third chapter of this book that the number one reason for recession in any nation is laziness. By that I mean the refusal of the citizens of that nation to become workaholics. Hence, for any country to develop, it has to first of all overcome the culture of laziness in its citizens by teaching them to become workaholics. The benefits of hard work were discussed in chapter four and among them is the fact that workaholics are always without equals in whatever they do. They stand out and take the place of honour above all else. Chapter five explained how hard work beats talent if talent doesn't work hard. In other words, talent is not enough; hard work is what makes the difference. Furthermore, I believe you understood from chapter six that everyone is in search of workaholics and that if you urgently become one, you will be in high demand. One striking thing you should not take for granted is the fact that with hard work, life is predictable. You do not need a prophet to predict your future if you are a workaholic. You can predict your own future and work out your miracles. In chapter eight, the emphasis was on your purpose and calling. When you want to become great, you have to become a workaholic in your area of purpose and calling instead of just living your life for a job description. In chapter nine, I highlighted the consequences of not becoming a workaholic. The life of anybody who is not a workaholic will be a life of constant pain and regrets. However to live a life without constant pain and regrets, you must urgently become a workaholic. In this chapter, I am going to be teaching you how to urgently become a workaholic. The solution to the problems of Nigeria and other third world countries can be resolved if the principles stated here in this chapter are applied. I urge you to read on till the end as this may be a journey to the end of poverty, lack, mediocrity and economic recession in your life and in your country.

WHEN WORK MEETS TIME.

When you get the combination of time and work you become a superhuman. These are the two greatest things God has given to us; time and work. God's greatest gifts to man are time and work. Don't ever go to a church where they are telling you not to work. You should run away from any church that tells you not to work and to just believe and wait for miracles. Any church that tells you that one day of favour is better than ten years of labour or work is actually killing and depriving you of one of the greatest gifts of God to man, the gift of work. Work is as important as time.

These are the two greatest wealth God has given to you. No greater wealth than these two things.

Time is wealth number one and work is wealth number two.

That is why God instituted work before the fall of Adam and Eve. That is why work is not a curse. Work was there before sin was committed. Work was there after man was created.

Because of the importance of work, the bible said in genesis chapter two; even though God had created the heavens and the earth, no plant could grow because there was no man to work the ground. In chapter one God said "Let the land produce vegetation: seed-bearing plants and trees on the land that bear fruit with seed in it, according to their various kinds." And it was so. The land produced vegetation: plants bearing seed according to their kinds and trees bearing fruit with seed in it according to their kinds" but all were on the ground and nothing could grow. Why didn't they grow up? Because there was no man to work. As long as there is no man to work, God cannot give birth to blessings. When there are no men to work, God withholds blessings. When there are no men to labor, heaven withholds blessings. Heaven withholds blessings when men are not ready to work. When men are not ready to work, God keeps his resources to himself. That was why God could not even give rain to the earth. He could not send rain to the earth because there was no man to work on the ground.

It is only through work that time could be converted into value chains. It is only through work that time is exploited. It is only through work that time could be tamed. Time is tamed by the instrumentality of work. Time is possessed and taken advantage of only through the vehicle of work. The instrument for converting the resource of time into valuable product is work. We convert time into products and services through work. Work is God's blessings to you. That is why you must never tolerate anybody seating idle beside you. You must never tolerate anyone seating idle. That is why the bible said he that does not work should not eat. That is why Jesus said "my father works hitherto" If God could work, if God could not afford not to work, if he could not afford the luxury of laziness, then you have no excuse not to work. Even heaven is working and the angels are working. The luxury of not working and sitting down in laziness could not be afforded by God himself. So man is not permitted not to work. Jesus said "because I see my father work, I too work" "I will work while it is day". Work is something that we must take advantage of. Only the wise take advantage of work. Because work is the only instrument through which time could be converted. And of course there are different kinds of works. There is mental work, there is physical work and there is spiritual work. So work is not just physical labour. Work could be mental work, physical work or spiritual work but without work time cannot be converted. Everything is created out of time. Your car was produced as a result of hundreds of people investing their time, coming to work eight hours a day and converting their time into a product called car. They gave eight hours of their life every day, each of them investing eight hours every day and that was how your car was produced. It was not only the people who assembled the car but those who also produced the metal, those who did the spraying, those who produced the tools and so on, all of them were investing their time. It is the time invested that resulted in the car. The same thing is true for an aeroplane. The same is true for a book. It is the time invested by somebody to get the knowledge that produces a book. It is the time invested by somebody to sit down to write that produces a book. Every product you see is a product of time converted. It is when time is tamed and converted that we have products. When time is purposefully used through work, we have a house. When time is purposefully converted through work, we have a computer, an iPad or any product you can think of. Therefore whenever work is combined with time, we have a product. A workaholic therefore must understand the importance of both work and time. That is why you must make sure that you are always working per time. It is only when you combine work and time that you become successful in life.

URGENTLY BECOME A WORKAHOLIC

Dear friends, there is an emergency! Our nation is fast collapsing and swimming in the pool of economic recession. The government does not seem to have the solution the people desire. The people are confused and do not know what else to do. Everybody is crying and complaining of hardship. Parents can no longer pay their wards school fees and hospital bills. Inflation has hit the market and the price of every single commodity is on the high side. There is severe hunger and starvation in the land. Everyone is looking for a way to survive but the people do not seem to know which way to go. The citizens have gone on a nation-wide protest yet that did not and cannot in any way be the solution. There seems to be no way out and for most of the youths, some have resorted to becoming armed robbers, others fraudsters and yet others prostitutes. Unfortunately, none of these positions can transform a nation's economy. Everyone has lost hope and cannot seem to believe that there is any possibility of a solution. But I am glad to announce to you through this book that there is a solution. Yes there is a solution! What then can be the solution? Well, that is the reason I have written this book. I am about to give the solution to the Nigeria's economic crisis and my solution to the problem is none other but to ask my people to "Urgently Become Workaholics" Yes the solution to the Nigerian economic problem is for everyone to urgently become workaholic. It is time we all stopped depending on the government for survival. It is time for everyone to take responsibility for his own survival and the only way to do that is for you and me to urgently become workaholics. There is no longer time to live an indolent lifestyle. It will be foolishness for you to still be sleeping like you used to. A little more sleep, a little more slumber, and a little folding of the arms to rest, shall invite poverty to your life and it will overtake you like an armed man. It is time to stop anything that does not look like hard work. This is not the time to fold your arms and relax. If you do, you and your children will die of hunger. Your life will be full of constant pain and regrets.

My call to everyone now is to become workaholics. You need to work harder than you used to. You need to convert all your vacations and resting days into working days. There is no other way to salvage the Nigerian economy than for everyone to become hard workers. Hard work is the only way to revitalize the economy. Nothing else can take its place.

"There is no substitute for hard work."

THOMAS EDISON

The first thing we need to do to salvage our economy is to first teach our people the importance of time and secondly teach them the importance of hard work. We must raise a campaign against the use of time for frivolities and irrelevant activities that do not add value to the citizens nor the nation as a whole. We must raise a campaign against laziness. People must be taught that it is better to go to work than to go to the cinema. It is better to be at the industry working than to go watch football at the sport centre. All non- productive activities must be brought to a halt if we desire to see our nation revive again. It is far better to go to work than to go for unending church services. Nigerians have gone to church for too long yet no results to show for that. We have prayed all kind of prayers, yet our nation is still in recession. The solution therefore is not prayers but diligence. Everyone must become a workaholic and do so urgently. If we all become workaholics, we will stop depending on the government for survival. We will stop hoping on miracles to develop our nation.

Do you know that amidst all the economic recession, those who have become workaholics are not affected? They have accrued so much wealth through hard work that the economy doesn't decide whether or not they will survive. An example of such a workaholic is the industrialist, Aliko Dangote.

WHERE ARE THE INDUSTRIALISTS?

Born in 1957, Dangote grew up in an entrepreneurial household in Kano State, Nigeria. He was raised Muslim and had been exposed to an upper-class lifestyle since his birth. Dangote's grandfather, Sanusi Dantata, was once named one of the wealthiest people living in Kano. He made his fortune by selling commodities such as oats and rice. Dantata became Dangote's guardian in 1965, following the death of his father.

Having spent much of his childhood with his grandfather, Dangote quickly became interested in the world of business. He once said, "I can remember when I was in primary school, I would go and buy cartons of sweets [sugar boxes] and I would start selling them just to make money. I was so interested in business, even at that time."

At age 21, Dangote graduated from Egypt's Al-Azhar University, one of Islam's prestigious universities. It was there the budding entrepreneur furthered his education in business. During an interview this year with Forbes, Dangote explained, "When you are raised by an entrepreneurial parent or grandparent, you pick that aspiration. It makes you be much more aggressive – to think anything is possible."

AN EMPIRE IS BORN

After graduating from college in 1977, Dangote managed to convince his uncle to lend him $3,000 to start a business. The funds from the loan allowed him to import soft commodities at wholesale prices from international suppliers. Two of his main imports were rice from Thailand and sugar from Brazil. He then sold those items in small quantities, and at a lucrative mark-up, to consumers in his village. The venture quickly became successful and turned into a cash cow. Dangote claims that on some of his best days, he was realizing a daily net profit of $10,000. That allowed him to repay his uncle in only three months.

In 1997, Dangote realized that acting as a middleman was a very costly endeavour, and so he built a plant to produce what he had been importing and selling for the previous 20 years. His company began to produce pasta, sugar, salt and flour. Around the same time, Dangote was awarded a state-owned cement company. Dangote significantly expanded the operations of the company in 2005 by constructing a multimillion-dollar manufacturing plant. The construction was financed with $319 million of Dangote's own money in addition to a $479 million loan from the World Bank International Finance Corporation.

Each of his manufacturing divisions has since been separated into different publicly traded companies. Dangote Sugar Refinery Plc., for example, was listed on the Nigerian Stock Exchange in 2007. As of September, the company's market cap was 82 billionNaira ($411 million). Dangote subsequently took his salt, flour and cement segments public. Those businesses became the National Salt Company of Nigeria Plc., Dangote Flour Mills Plc., and Dangote Cements Plc., respectively.

Dear friends, I believe you've seen how Dangote grew to become an industrialist. There is almost no one in Africa who is a greater industrialist than him. He is a Nigerian and grew up in the same country that you and I were born. His love for hard work has set him apart from every other Nigerian. Not even the president or senators are as wealthy as he is. His secret to such greatness is none other than the fact that he is a workaholic. Most people think that it is because he grew up in a wealthy family that he became the richest black man in the world. I beg to disagree with that ideology. There are many other people who grew up in wealthy homes too but did not multiply their wealth through hard work and hence could not attain the status that Dangote has attained. I could proof to you that it was hard work that made him the Dangote that we all celebrate today. To proof that, I want us to consider some of his words:

> *I enjoy myself a lot but I derive more joy in working. I believe in hard work and one of my business success secrets is hard work. It's hard to see a youth that will go to bed by 2am and wake up by 5am. I don't rest until I achieve something."*
>
> ### ALIKO DANGOTE

Dear friends, did you just read that? I am sure it is obvious from the very words of Dangote himself that it was hard work that took him to the top. No one can argue the fact that he is a workaholic. What can our youths learn from this great man? The number one thing we need to revive a nation's economy full of lazy people is to begin to awaken a consciousness of hard work in our youths. Every youth must urgently become a workaholic. Instead of just wishing that wealth will come to you, start learning the principles of hard work. Every one of us must stop sleeping like all is well when it is obvious that we are all dying of hunger and starvation. We must urgently become workaholics. We must all become industrious citizens.

EXPANDING THE EMPIRE

Dangote has always reinvested the majority of his profits back into his businesses, which is one reason the company has grown so much since inception. During an interview with Al Jazeera News, he explained, "we [Dangote Group] are not doing like other Africans who keep most of their money in the bank. We do not keep money in bank. We fully invest whatever we have and we keep on investing."

Dangote has also recently entered the oil and gas industry, a sector that he purposely avoided for most of his career. Unlike many wealthy Nigerians who made their fortune in oil, Dangote chose to go down a different path. "If we [Dangote Group] had followed the trend of dealing with oil, we would have tainted our name. People would have thought 'You [Dangote] made so much money because you did a lot of unethical dealings in the oil industry," he said once.

In an effort to put some of his cash reserves to work, Dangote purchased an oil refinery in Lagos in 2007. He hopes that the refinery, which is scheduled to be commissioned in the third quarter of 2017, will significantly reduce Nigeria's reliance on international suppliers for oil and gas. The plant is expected to produce half a million barrels of oil a day

Dear friends, the richest man in Africa has given us an advice during his interview with Aljazeera and that advice is that we must all learn to invest our money into businesses instead of keeping it in the bank. I therefore submit that the way to revive our dying economy is to raise a generation of industrialist who will work hard and invest their money into industrialization. If Dangote does that and it works for him, then I think everyone of us should do the same. If we could all first of all make up our minds to become industrialists and then secondly invest our money into our industries, we would soon realize that our dying economy will begin to rise again.

My question therefore is; where are the industrialists in our nation? Where are the workaholics? Our nation is in a state of recession because we lack industrialists and workaholics. My call therefore to the citizens of my nation is to become workaholics and industrialists. My call to my fellow men is to follow the footstep of Africa's richest man and by so doing we would turn our nation from a developing country to an industrialized and a developed nation.

AN INDUSTRIAL REVOLUTION IN NIGERIA

Dear friends my solution to the Nigerian economic problem is that we cause an industrial revolution in the nation and the way to do that is to first raise workaholics and industrialists. If you and I set up factories and small scale businesses all across the nation, we would have everybody employed and no one will be roaming the streets looking for a government job. That means that every street in Nigeria is littered with industries, businesses and factories. By so doing, we would all become workaholics and industrialists and we would raise over a million Dangotes' in Nigeria. It is time we stopped importation of commodities from other countries. We all should begin to manufacture one product or the other. When that happens we would become an exporting country rather than an importing one. That was one of the secrets of Dangote. For many years, Dangote imported soft commodities and resold them in his community. He eventually ceased importing items and began to manufacture his own products. Over the years, Dangote has expanded into new business segments, including telecommunications, real estate and steel manufacturing. Today his holding company, Dangote Group, is the largest conglomerate in West Africa.

Beloved friends, looking at the life of Africa's richest man I want to challenge you to begin to work hard, begin to think industry, and begin to think hard work. Africa's richest man sleeps only 3hours a day!!! What are you doing with your life? Do you want to sleep away your life and the future of your unborn children? If you refuse to become a workaholic, you will be putting the lives of unborn generations in danger. You will have nothing to leave for the next generation. If you however decide to become a workaholic and an industrialist, I want you to know that you can become as rich as Dangote but that will not happen all of a sudden. It will take repeated hard work, dedication and time, but the good news is that it will eventually happen. Dangote himself did not become rich all of a sudden. It took some time, hard work and dedication.

"I built a conglomerate and emerged the richest black man in the world in 2008 but it didn't happen overnight. It took me thirty years to get to where I am today. Youths of today aspire to be like me but they want to achieve it overnight. It's not going to work. To build a successful business, you must start small and dream big. In the journey of entrepreneurship, tenacity of purpose is supreme."

ALIKO DANGOTE

Do you want to become an industrialist? If yes, then I want you to emulate the life of Aliko Dangote. I want you to emulate his hard work. Become a workaholic like him. The harder you work the luckier you get. Become an investor like him. Dangote once said:

> *"After my death, I want to be remembered as Africa's greatest industrialist."*

My question to you therefore is: "What do you want to be remembered for?" Do you want to be recognised and remembered as the one who caused an industrial revolution in Nigeria? Do you want to be numbered among those who put an end to the economic recession in your country? If your answer is yes, then you must urgently become a workaholic. You will need to urgently become an industrialist. When you become an industrialist, you will become a problem solver and a solution provider.

> *"Every morning when I wake up, I make up my mind to solve as many problems, before retiring home."*
>
> ALIKO DANGOTE

Dangote thinks of how he can solve humanity's problems. Dangote boosted local cement production, plummeted cement importation and reduced cement congestion at Nigerian ports. Now, he just slashed cement cost by 50 percent! Are you seeking to just enrich yourself without thinking of how to solve the market's problems? If your answer is in the affirmative, you need to learn from Africa's biggest industrialist. He knows better!

Having read the story of Aliko Dangote, let's now list the characteristics that defined the man that you and I can emulate.

- He is a workaholic
- He is a hard worker
- He is an industrialist
- He is business minded
- He knows the value of time
- He doesn't sleep away his time
- He is an investor
- He is a problem solver

NUGGETS FROM
CHAPTER TEN

1. When you get the combination of time and work you become a superhuman.

2. God's greatest gifts to man are time and work.

3. You should run away from any church that tells you not to work and to just believe and wait for miracles.

4. Any church that tells you that one day of favour is better than ten years of labour or work is actually killing and depriving you of one of the greatest gifts of God to man, the gift of work.

5. Time is wealth number one and work is wealth number two.

6. As long as there is no man to work, God cannot give birth to blessings. When there are no men to work, God withholds blessings. When there are no men to labor, heaven withholds blessings. Heaven withholds blessings when men are not ready to work. When men are not ready to work, God keeps his resources to himself

7. It is only through work that time could be converted into value chains. It is only through work that time is exploited. It is only through work that time could be tamed.

8. The instrument for converting the resource of time into valuable product is work.

9. The luxury of not working and sitting down in laziness could not be afforded by God himself. So man is not permitted not to work.

10. Whenever work is combined with time, we have a product. A workaholic therefore must understand the importance of both work and time.

PRINCIPLES FROM
CHAPTER TEN

1. The solution to the Nigerian economic problem is for everyone to urgently become workaholics.

2. It is time for everyone to take responsibility for his own survival and the only way to do that is for you and me to urgently become workaholics.

3. There is no other way to salvage the Nigerian economy than for everyone to become hard workers

4. Hard work is the only way to revitalize the economy. Nothing else can take its place.

5. The first thing we need to do to salvage our economy is to first teach our people the importance of time and secondly teach them the importance of hard work.

6. We must raise a campaign against laziness. People must be taught that it is better to go to work than to go to the cinema

7. All non- productive activities must be brought to a halt if we desire to see our nation revive again.

8. If we all become workaholics, we will stop depending on the government for survival. We will stop hoping on miracles to develop our nation.

9. The number one thing we need to revive a nation's economy full of lazy people is to begin to awaken a consciousness of hard work in our youths.

10. Instead of just wishing that wealth will come to you, start learning the principles of hard work.

CONCLUSION

Dear friends, I do hope you will apply the principles that are in this book. It is my desire that you become a workaholic and work hard to succeed in life. I sincerely believe that you can become financially wealthy, you can become successful in life, you can become a champion and you can become great. My only prayer is that you will not trivialize the principles that I have given to you in this book but that you will apply them to eliminate any form of laziness from your life and work yourself up to greatness and prominence. It is my prayer also that Nigeria, Africa and all other under-developed nations will apply the principles in this book and use them to elevate their nations from third world to first world countries.

Finally, dear friends, if you forget anything in this book do not forget the central idea of this book which is "Urgently Become A Workaholic" I encourage you to resolve to become a workaholic because it is only through hard work can you truly become great in life. Go and live the life of a workaholic and I am sure sooner than you think, the world will see you at the top. Good Luck!

For The Love Of God, Church And Nation.
Dr. Sunday Adelaja

EPILOGUE

Congratulations for coming to the end of this book! I know that it has been a life transforming journey for you. You have seen that regaining your lost years is not only a possibility but I trust that you have actually started the process by practicing all you have been learning.

We have seen that a wrong attitude to time is one of the major reasons why people mismanage time. Time is our greatest earthly possession and it has to be valued and protected from time killers. We have seen several habits that are time killers but the advent of social media has worsened the situation. Hours are spent on social media without any resultant positive results. It is absolutely important to put a restriction on the amount of time spent on social media, TV, social activities etc.

You have been given time-proven principles that will help you to reclaim your lost years. These principles were employed by individuals and nations and will produce the same results in your life if you would commit to practicing them.

As reiterated many times, the key to regaining your lost years is investing maximum value into every second and hour of the day. This will ensure that you produce more results within each hour unlike before.

Amongst the principles discussed in this book, the single and most important one that will restore your lost years is Intensity. The practice of being intense towards any task will bring about speedy results. The habit of intensity was responsible for the success of the Asian tigers in developing their economy from third world nation to first world within a few decades.

But to accelerate the process of reclaiming your lost years, it is imperative to combine more qualities together rather than intensity alone. There are three qualities when combined produce the highest benefits; they are Speed, Focus and Intensity.

Whatever you wish to produce, either value to your life or others, goods or services, the inclusion of these three qualities will triple your speed and increase your results. Every activity that is targeted towards the attainment of your goals must be done with Speed, Focus and Intensity. Whether it involves work, solitude, self-education, it should be engaged in with speed, focus and intensity in order to yield maximum results. These keys will help you to regain your lost years.

So as earlier said, you hold in your hands, the keys and strategies that will enable you regain your lost years. The rest depends on you. I would like to remind you once again on how to get the best out of this book. These were discussed in detail at the beginning of the book.

To ensure that you redeem your lost years, go back and read this book again. Read it out loud and underline the important points and ideas found in the book. Then re-read the underlined points and begin immediately to practice what you learnt. Secondly pay attention to the nuggets and exercises discussed in the conclusion section. Put them to practice immediately.

These will ensure that this book is not just one more book amongst your list rather, a book that transformed your life and helped you to regain your lost years.

REFERENCES

Chapter 1 • Can I Regain My Lost Years?

1. Pewtrust.org, "The Impact of the September 2008 Economic Collapse", April 28, 2010, *http://www.pewtrusts.org/en/research-and-analysis/reports/2010/04/28/the-impact-of-the-september-2008-economic-collapse* (accessed November 9, 2016).

2. "The effects of Hurricane Katrina on New Orleans Economy", Monthly Labour Review, June 2007, *http://www.bls.gov/opub/mlr/2007/06/art1full.pdf* (accessed November 9, 2016).

3. USlegal.com, "Profiles of famous/newsworthy bankruptcies", *https://bankruptcy.uslegal.com/profilesfamousbankruptcies/walt-disney/* (accessed November 9, 2016).

4. Biography.com, "Colonel Harland Sanders Biography", *http://www.biography.com/people/colonel-harland-sanders-12353545* (accessed November 9, 2016).

Chapter 2 • Time, Our Greatest Treasure

1. Kane L. June 26, 2014, "9 things rich people do and don't do everyday", *http://www.businessinsider.com/rich-people-daily-habits-2014-6* (accessed November 12, 2016).

Chapter 5 • Learn To Say "No"

1. Go-globe.com, "Social Media Addiction- Statistics and Trends", *http://www.go-globe.com/blog/social-media-addiction/* (accessed, November 10, 2016).

2. Wallace K., (2015, November 3), "Teens spend a 'mind-boggling' 9 hours a day using media, report says", *http://www.cnn.com/2015/11/03/health/teens-tweens-media-screen-use-report/* (accessed, November 10, 2016).

Chapter 7 • Be Intense

1. Nytimes.com, (2015, October 10), "The Asian Advantage", *http://www.nytimes.com/2015/10/11/opinion/sunday/the-asian-advantage.html?_r=1* (accessed , November 2016).

2. Todayonline.com, "Singapore world's most expensive city third year row says eiu report", a *http://www.todayonline.com/singapore/singapore-worlds-most-expensive-city-third-year-row-says-eiu-report* (accessed November 22, 2016).

3. Topuniversities.com, "Faculty rankings arts and humanities, humanities, *http://www.topuniversities.com/university-rankings/faculty-rankings/arts-and-humanities/2015* (accessed November 22, 2016).

4. Newshub.nus.edu.sg, "NUS attains 11th spot in the Financial Times Executive MBA 2009 rankings", October 19th 2009, *http://newshub.nus.edu.sg/headlines/1009/ranking_19Oct09.php*, (accessed November 22, 2016).

5. Pwc.com, "Cities of opportunities" *http://www.pwc. com/us/en/cities-of-opportunity/2014/assets/cities-of- opportunity-2014.pdf,* (accessed November 22, 2016).

6. Investopedia.com, "The world's Top 10 economies", July18, 2016, *http://www.investopedia.com/ articles/investing/022415/worlds-top-10- economies.asp,* (accessed November 22, 2016).

7. Kleiner, JüRgen (2001). Korea, **A Century of Change.** ISBN 978-981-02-4657-0. *https://books.google. com/books?id=nTCC2ZheFu0C&pg=PA254&lpg =PA254&dq=han+river+miracle&q=han+river+ miracle&hl=en#v=snippet&q=han%20river%20 miracle&f=false* (Accessed November 22, 2016).

Chapter 10 • Conversion Through Hard Work

1. Forbes.com, "The Sleep Habits of Highly Successful People" November 13, 2015, *http://www.forbes.com/ sites/alicegwalton/2015/11/13/the-sleep-habits-of- highly-successful-people-infographic/#6c9e79fb386f,* (accessed November 22, 2016).

INFORMATION ABOUT
THE EMBASSY OF GOD CHURCH
AND PASTOR SUNDAY ADELAJA

Pastor Sunday Adelaja — The only black man in the world that leads a congregation of mostly Caucasians in 50 countries. Below are some facts about Pastor Sunday's life and ministry.

- Pastor Sunday is the pastor of the largest Evangelical Church in Europe with a population of 99.9% white Europeans in Kiev Ukraine.
- His ministry has charity units that feed over 5000 people on a daily basis.
- Through his ministry over 30 thousand people have been delivered from drug and alcohol addictions.
- He helped raise over 200 millionaires in US dollars in his church, most of whom were former drug/ alcohol addicts and societal outcasts.
- He has raised a global movement that is influencing over 70 million people around the globe.
- Branches of his church are in over 50 countries.
- He has spoken in different nations of the world on National Transformation.
- Pastor Sunday is one of the few, if not the only African, who has ever spoken in the US senate.
- Pastor Sunday is one of the few African pastors who has spoken on the floor of the UN.
- He has addressed the Japanese Members of parliament.
- He has spoken in the Knesset to members of Israeli parliament. The list goes on and on.
- His ministry has over 500 hundred government officials holding different government positions in Ukraine.
- He has written and published over 300 books and recorded thousands of messages.

THE EMBASSY OF GOD CHURCH

There are more than 300 rehabilitation centers for alcohol and drug addicts which have been operational in Ukraine and Europe since 1994.

More than 20 000 people recovered from their addictions, and became normal members of the society. Thanks to the rehabilitation centers opened by the church.

There are homes for abandoned street children operated by the church which have successfully reunited more than 5 000 children with their families.

The Embassy of God Church is involved in many social projects that are directed at maintaining family values, active civil involvement and individual fulfillment of church members.

Many former members of mafia organizations and criminals have become devout Christians through the missionary work of the Embassy of God Church.

The church's hot-line has counseled over a 200,000 people.

Right now there are over 25,000 members in the Embassy of God Church Kyiv, Ukraine.

BIOGRAPHY OF PASTOR SUNDAY ADELAJA

Pastor Sunday Adelaja is the Founder and Senior Pastor of The Embassy of the Blessed Kingdom of God for All Nations Church in Kyiv, Ukraine.

He is a Nigerian-born leader with an apostolic gift for the twenty-first century. In his mid thirties Pastor Sunday had already proven to be one of the world's most dynamic communicators and church planters and is regarded as the most successful pastor in Europe with over 25,000 members as well as daughter and satellite churches in over 50 countries worldwide.

The congregation includes members from all spheres of society, from former drug and alcohol addicts, to politicians and millionaires. It's high percentage of white Europeans (99%), also indicates that boundaries of racial prejudice have been surpassed. In the same country where Pastor Sunday was called "chocolate rabbit" and several attempts have been made to deport him, thousands join hands and support his mission to see Ukraine and the whole world affected and saved by the gospel of the Kingdom. Pastor Sunday is recognized as an unusually gifted teacher of the Word of God, with an extraordinary operation in the gifts of the Spirit, especially the word of knowledge. He receives numerous speaking invitations to several countries in all continents of the world yearly, as well as invitations to meetings with heads of States and other Politicians.

Pastor Sunday's influence in the areas of church growth, prayer and evangelism has been noted by Charisma Magazine, Ministries Today and many other Christian periodicals. The secular world media, such as the Wall Street Journal, Forbes, Washington Post, Reuters, Associated Press, CNN, BBC and German, Dutch and French national television have all widely reported on him. The Wall Street Journal called him "A Man with a Mission" set out to save Kyiv. The Ukrainian President Yushenko acknowledged his strong involvement in the Orange revolution for democracy in Ukraine. Former Mayor of New York City Rudolph Giuliani stated: "Sunday, God bless you in your important mission. When I next come to Ukraine I would like to be at your church".

In August 2007 by invitation from the employees of the UN, Pastor Sunday Adelaja was invited as a speaker for three sessions. It was the first time in the history of the UN that a pastor speaks in the main hall of the UN. There were 500 organizations and missions from different parts of the world and leaders from 30 countries that participated in these sessions. From then on, the Embassy of God started its preparation to enter the UN and become a member of this organization.

Pastor Sunday's passion for National Transformation has driven him to maximally spread the word of God. He has written and published over 200 books of which some have been translated to English, German, Chinese, Arabic and Dutch. Also, thousands of sermons have been recorded. He organizes annual pastors leadership seminars where over 1,000 ministers regularly attend, studying the topic 'Pastoring without Tears'. His passion is to ignite these ministers with fire and power to transform their cities and countries.

Every year Pastor Sunday organizes Pastor's Seminars that take place in the church. He is also the main speaker there. During this time more than 1 000 Ministers learn how to be a pastor without tears, and learn the keys of achieving success. Also, every year Pastor Sunday organizes a summer and winter fast which aims at equipping Ministers with fire and power to change their cities and countries.

Nowadays, the apostolic ministry of Pastor Sunday has gone far beyond the boundaries of Ukraine, making him a desirable speaker and a Pastor to Pastors in many nations of the world. To date, he has visited over 50 countries.

Pastor Sunday is happily married to his "Princess" Abosede, and they are blessed with three children: Perez, Zoe and Pearl.

Below is the link to a photo gallery of Pastor Sunday and other likeminded individuals who have also positively impacted their nations:

http://www.godembassy.com/media/photo/view-album/3.html

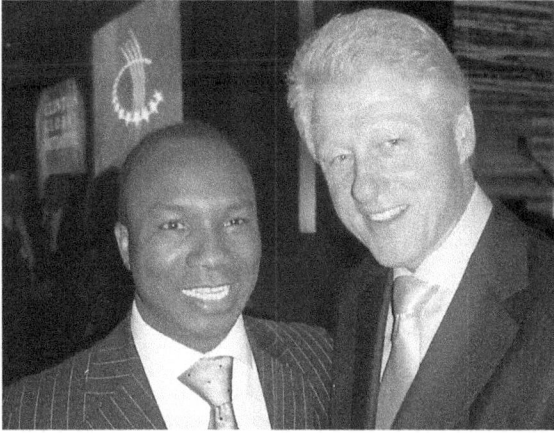

Bill Clinton —
42Nd President Of The
United States (1993–2001),
Former Arcansas State
Governor

Ariel "Arik" Sharon —
Israeli Politician, Israeli
Prime Minister (2001–2006)

Benjamin Netanyahu —
Statesman Of Israel. Israeli
Prime Minister (1996–1999),
Acting Prime Minister
(From 2009)

Jean ChrEtien —
Canadian Politician,
20Th Prime Minister Of
Canada, Minister Of Justice
Of Canada, Head Of Liberan
Party Of Canada

Rudolph Giuliani —
American Political Actor,
Mayor Of New York Served
From 1994 To 2001. Actor
Of Republican Party

Colin Powell —
Is An American Statesman
And A Retired Four-Star
General In The Us Army,
65Th United States Secretary
Of State

Peter J. Daniels —
Is A Well-Known And
Respected Australian
Christian International
Business Statesman Of
Substance

**Madeleine
Korbel Albright** —
An American Politician And
Diplomat, 64[Th] United States
Secretary Of State

**Kenneth Robert
Livingstone** —
An English Politician,
1[St] Mayor Of London
(4 May 2000 – 4 May
2008), Labour Party
Representative

Sir Richard Charles Nicholas Branson — English Business Magnate, Investor And Philanthropist. He Founded The *Virgin Group*, Which Controls More Than 400 Companies

Mel Gibson — American Actor And Filmmaker

Chuck Norris — American Martial Artist, Actor, Film Producer And Screenwriter

Christopher Tucker — American Actor And Comedian

Bernice Albertine King — American Minister Best Known As The Youngest Child Of Civil Rights Leaders Martin Luther King Jr. And Coretta Scott King Andrew

Andrew Young — American Politician, Diplomat, And Activist, 14Th United States Ambassador To The United Nations, 55Th Mayor Of Atlanta

General Wesley Kanne Clark — 4-Star General And Nato Supreme Allied Commander

Dr. Sunday Adelaja's family: Perez, Pearl, Zoe and Pastor Bose Adelaja

FOLLOW
SUNDAY ADELAJA
ON SOCIAL MEDIA

Subscribe And Read Pastor Sunday's Blog:
www.sundayadelajablog.com

**Follow these links and listen to over 200
of Pastor Sunday's Messages free of charge:**
http://sundayadelajablog.com/content/

Follow Pastor Sunday on Twitter:
www.twitter.com/official_pastor

Join Pastor Sunday's Facebook page to stay in touch:
www.facebook.com/pastor.sunday.adelaja

**Visit our websites for more information
about Pastor Sunday's ministry:**
http://www.godembassy.com
http://www.pastorsunday.com
http://sundayadelaja.de

CONTACT

FOR DISTRIBUTION OR TO ORDER
BULK COPIES OF THIS BOOK,
PLEASE CONTACT US:

USA
CORNERSTONE PUBLISHING
info@thecornerstonepublishers.com
+1 (516) 547-4999
www.thecornerstonepublishers.com

AFRICA
SUNDAY ADELAJA MEDIA LTD.
E-mail: btawolana@hotmail.com
+2348187518530, +2348097721451, +2348034093699

LONDON, UK
PASTOR ABRAHAM GREAT
abrahamagreat@gmail.com
+447711399828, +441908538141

KIEV, UKRAINE
pa@godembassy.org
Mobile: +380674401958

BEST SELLING BOOKS BY DR. SUNDAY ADELAJA
AVAILABLE ON AMAZON.COM AND OKADABOOKS.COM

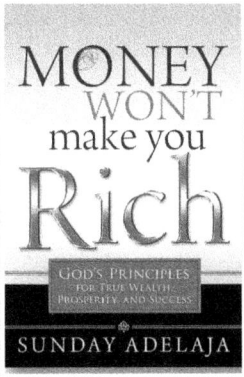

MONEY WON'T make you **Rich**
GOD'S PRINCIPLES FOR TRUE WEALTH, PROSPERITY, AND SUCCESS
SUNDAY ADELAJA

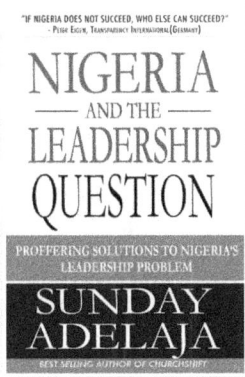

"IF NIGERIA DOES NOT SUCCEED, WHO ELSE CAN SUCCEED?"
- PETER EIGEN, TRANSPARENCY INTERNATIONAL (GERMANY)

NIGERIA — AND THE — **LEADERSHIP QUESTION**
PROFFERING SOLUTIONS TO NIGERIA'S LEADERSHIP PROBLEM
SUNDAY ADELAJA
BEST SELLING AUTHOR OF CHURCHSHIFT

MYLES MUNROE
... FINDING ANSWERS TO WHY GOOD PEOPLE DIE TRAGIC AND EARLY DEATHS
SUNDAY ADELAJA

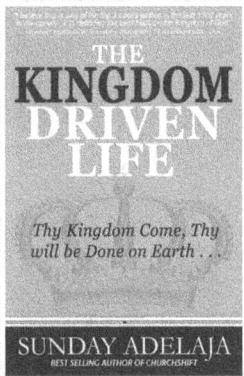

THE KINGDOM DRIVEN LIFE
Thy Kingdom Come, Thy will be Done on Earth . . .
SUNDAY ADELAJA
BEST SELLING AUTHOR OF CHURCHSHIFT

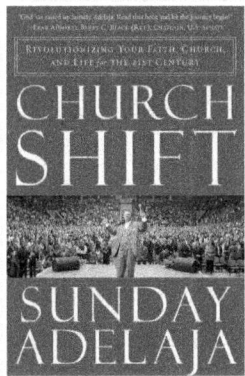

REVOLUTIONIZING YOUR FAITH, CHURCH, AND LIFE for THE 21ST CENTURY
CHURCH SHIFT
SUNDAY ADELAJA

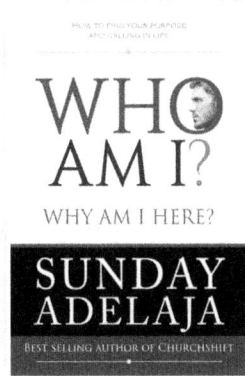

HOW TO FIND YOUR PURPOSE AND CALLING IN LIFE
WHO AM I?
WHY AM I HERE?
SUNDAY ADELAJA
BEST SELLING AUTHOR OF CHURCHSHIFT

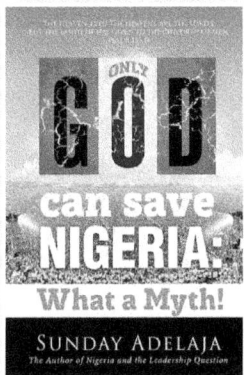

ONLY **GOD** can save **NIGERIA:** What a Myth!
SUNDAY ADELAJA
The Author of Nigeria and the Leadership Question

BEST SELLING 10 TIMES
MONEY IS A GOOD SLAVE, BUT A BAD MASTER
IF YOU ARE WORKING FOR MONEY YOU ARE UNDER UNCLE SAM SYSTEM. YOU NEED TO GET OUT FAST. THIS BOOK WILL HELP YOU DO IT.
STOP **WORKING** FOR **UNCLE SAM**
SUNDAY ADELAJA

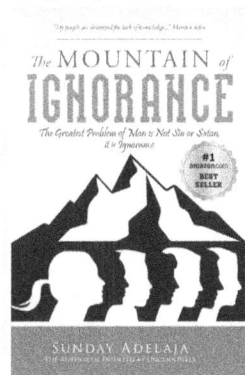

The **MOUNTAIN** of **IGNORANCE**
The Greatest Problem of Man is Not Sin or Satan, it is Ignorance
#1 AMAZON.COM BEST SELLER
SUNDAY ADELAJA

BEST SELLING BOOKS BY DR. SUNDAY ADELAJA
AVAILABLE ON AMAZON.COM AND OKADABOOKS.COM

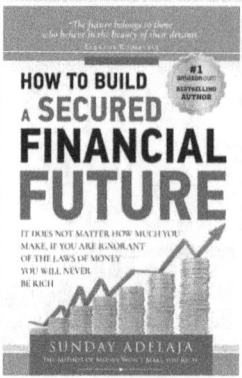

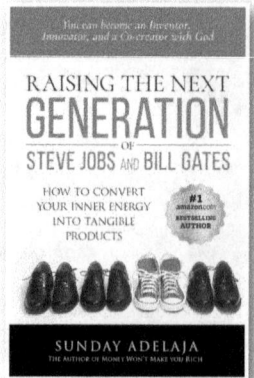

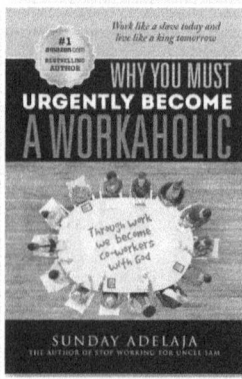

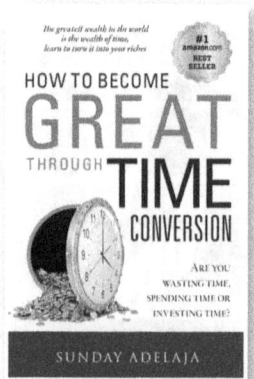

OLORUNWA

INSULTED by UNGODLINESS
RAISING A GENERATION OF THE PROVOKED IN EVERY NATION
SUNDAY ADELAJA
BEST SELLING AUTHOR OF CHURCHSHIFT

HOW TO REGAIN YOUR LOST YEARS
#1 AMAZON.COM BESTSELLING AUTHOR
SUNDAY ADELAJA

HOW TO BUILD A SECURED FINANCIAL FUTURE
#1 AMAZON.COM BESTSELLING AUTHOR
IT DOES NOT MATTER HOW MUCH YOU MAKE, IF YOU ARE IGNORANT OF THE LAWS OF MONEY YOU WILL NEVER BE RICH
SUNDAY ADELAJA
THE AUTHOR OF MONEY WON'T MAKE YOU RICH

Every man has a worth not every man has a net worth
#1 AMAZON.COM BESTSELLING AUTHOR
YOUR MONEY IS TEMPORARY, YOUR NET WORTH IS ETERNAL.
CREATE YOUR OWN NET WORTH
SUNDAY ADELAJA
THE AUTHOR OF MONEY WON'T MAKE YOU RICH

You can become an Inventor, Innovator, and a Co-creator with God
RAISING THE NEXT GENERATION OF STEVE JOBS AND BILL GATES
HOW TO CONVERT YOUR INNER ENERGY INTO TANGIBLE PRODUCTS
#1 AMAZON.COM BESTSELLING AUTHOR
SUNDAY ADELAJA
THE AUTHOR OF MONEY WON'T MAKE YOU RICH

REAL POVERTY IS NOT IN THE SIZE OF YOUR POCKET BUT IN THE SIZE OF YOUR MIND
POVERTY MINDSET VS ABUNDANCE MINDSET
#1 AMAZON.COM BEST SELLER
SUNDAY ADELAJA
THE AUTHOR OF MONEY WON'T MAKE YOU RICH

Work like a slave today and live like a king tomorrow
#1 AMAZON.COM BESTSELLING AUTHOR
WHY YOU MUST URGENTLY BECOME A WORKAHOLIC
Through work we become Co-workers with God
SUNDAY ADELAJA
THE AUTHOR OF STOP WORKING FOR UNCLE SAM

The greatest wealth in the world is the wealth of time, learn to turn it into your riches
#1 AMAZON.COM BEST SELLER
HOW TO BECOME GREAT THROUGH TIME CONVERSION
ARE YOU WASTING TIME, SPENDING TIME OR INVESTING TIME?
SUNDAY ADELAJA

GOLDEN JUBILEE SERIES BOOKS
BY DR. SUNDAY ADELAJA

FOR DISTRIBUTION OR TO ORDER BULK COPIES OF THIS BOOKS, PLEASE CONTACT US:

USA | CORNERSTONE PUBLISHING
E-mail: info@thecornerstonepublishers.com, +1 (516) 547-4999
www.thecornerstonepublishers.com

AFRICA | SUNDAY ADELAJA MEDIA LTD.
E-mail: btawolana@hotmail.com
+2348187518530, +2348097721451, +2348034093699

LONDON, UK | PASTOR ABRAHAM GREAT
E-mail: abrahamagreat@gmail.com, +447711399828, +441908538141

KIEV, UKRAINE |
E-mail: pa@godembassy.org, Mobile: +380674401958